Who Is
Jane Marshall?

Eileen Fox

Published by Dolman Scott in 2024

Copyright © 2024 Eileen Fox

All rights reserved. No part of this publication may be reproduced, stored in a retrieval system, or transmitted in any form or by any means, electronic, mechanical, photocopy, recording or otherwise, without prior written permission of the copyright owner. Nor can it be circulated in any form of binding or cover other than that in which it is published and without similar condition including this condition being imposed on a subsequent purchaser.

ISBN 978-1-915351-35-7

Published by

www.dolmanscott.com

For my mum, who's love and sense of humour, – the love she had for her own parents and siblings, helped form my character.

Many thanks to my son Peter for being the first to "check over my book". Thanks also to Pat Beaumont for reading my story and for being honest and positive.
Thank you to my daughter for putting up with me all of these years. She has been an amazing support when memories of my past overcame me. Thankfully not too often, as I mostly put my early years behind me.
A special thank you to Amy for getting me over the line with this book.

Contents

Chapter One	1
Chapter Two	7
Chapter Three	11
Chapter Four	19
Chapter Five	25
Chapter Six	33
Chapter Seven	41
Chapter Eight	45
Chapter Nine	51
Chapter Ten	57
Chapter Eleven	69
Chapter Twelve	77
Chapter Thirteen	85
Chapter Fourteen	91
Chapter Fifteen	103
Chapter Sixteen	109
Chapter Seventeen	115
Chapter Eighteen	125
Chapter Nineteen	131
Chapter Twenty	141

Who Is Jane Marshall?

My story begins with me at the age of eighteen, leaving my roots in the north of England, and giving flashbacks to a childhood which gave me so much, but which was also at times a painful existence.

Once I left home and eventually moved South, I met a young man whose family became a thread in my life story, even though he was only with me for twelve years.

Chapter One

I felt nervous, and excited at the same time. As my train pulled out of Darlington station, headed for a small market town named Hitchin, just north of London, I was at eighteen starting a whole new life. Away from past upsets, friends, sadness, and heading to what seemed to me, a kinder, softer place.

I had already left home, during the night, the very day of my 18th birthday. I had received a couple of cards, gone to work, then completed my plans for leaving home with my work colleagues. This experience was one of many fear driven moments which I had endured up to this point in my life. I had one more trial to get through after this, then it would be six months more before I would feel true freedom.

The train rocked and clicked its way further South. I felt my mind and body relax.

At an interview in an office in Darlington, my two interviewers, a married couple, seemed to like me and they explained the job on offer clearly. They told me that my accommodation would be provided, and also that I would receive a better wage than I was presently on, being as we would be near to London. Five days later I received a letter confirming that I was successful and I was offered the job. So here I was on the train, heading South, for a new start in life

My present landlady and her husband, who had been so kind to me since renting me their spare room, quite near to where I left home,- cried. I cried too! They were about sixty years old as far as I could tell, and had no children of their own. Their warmth and kindness towards me had been incredible. After one week of living with them, they began making me sandwiches for lunch, and also doing my washing for free.

At that time, I worked for a furniture manufacturer in Newton Aycliffe, as an office girl. I made notes regarding any returns of furniture, and I planned the driver's routes around the UK. Well, I helped with that, as so many of the towns and villages on the delivery requests, I had heard of, but I had no idea where they were.

My wage of five pounds, twelve shillings each week, meant that I had to walk half a mile to and from work each day, pay five pounds for my room and buy a "Jim's pie" (minced beef in rich gravy) for lunch, for one shilling a day. That left seven shillings to save per week. When I first started work at sixteen, my wage had been less than five pounds. My mum always opened my wage packet and gave me back enough money for bus fare and a pie for lunch.

Now that my landlady was making me sandwiches for my lunch, and I lived closer to work since moving, this gave me twelve shillings to save each week. Less than a pound.

Once I had saved seven pounds, I caught the bus into Darlington on a Saturday morning. I saw a beige herringbone coat for six pounds in Dorothy Perkins. I bought it. Then I was lucky enough to find some flat brown shoes for one pound, in the sale, at another shop. I had been using a coat given to me by friends since leaving my family home.

When I had moved quietly, hardly breathing, downstairs to the front door, I had not dared to put a coat on.

In case I was stopped, I could say I had not undressed for bed yet, and was getting some water. I had given a small carrier bag of clothes to my friends the previous day so that I could literally just grab my handbag and go.

As it happened, it all seemed too easy, no-one heard me leave, they were watching the tv. I closed the front door quietly, I could see a car across the road, warning lights blinking, I began to run. Breathlessly, I threw myself into the car, my heart beating fast. The two girls who had come to pick me up, said "It's clear, you're fine."

The sun was making me squint at the passing scenery, the motion of the train lulled me into a gentle nap. I was back in the car, one of my friends was driving, the other was holding my hand. Wonderful girls who had seen my fear when I talked of not being able to go out with them for drinks, or dinner, or blind dates. They had seen me shake when I talked about my parents' violent arguments. I never told them that at a mere three and a half years old, I had stood between mum and dad begging for my naked mother not to go outside. My father's face was red and angry, as he was threatening her, I said "you won't hit her will you?" he said "No", mum hesitated, and in that second he punched her straight in her face.

Her nose broke, she screamed. "That's your fault," she said looking down at my horrified, trembling body. I never got over it, even today, some seventy years later, I cry at the memory. My mum's poor eyes were black and blue, she hid away for ages.

I also never told these wonderful friends of when, at some seven or eight years of age, I had answered my father back. He leapt up from the floor, terror made me turn and run. I ran out of the house, out of the garden, along the track leading to the farmer's field. I crossed one field, then the second, a third, then I was coming up to the railway line, I threw myself down the bank and gripped the grass desperately trying to quiet my rushed breathing.

As I dared to look up, I could see his head and chest. "Please don't let him see me", I thought. He turned and probably left, but I daren't look for a long time. I lay and just cried, as quietly as I could. I was in a state of fear for some hours, and wrestling with the fact that I had to go home. I had to face whatever came, and it was getting dark. To be fair my father was probably now worried about me, he probably knew he'd frightened me, because when I crept back in and went to my bedroom, he knew, but he didn't come near. We never spoke of what happened, but I never forgot.

So my friends at work, who on my birthday helped me to leave, acted purely on the state of me rather than anything I said.

These incidents of violence were the ones that affected me, but the shouting and arguments were weekly, affecting my other siblings not to mention the neighbours. Banging doors, screaming, and every day walking past the houses in our village to catch the school bus. Thankfully, there were many very happy family days too, when laughter filled the house. Comedy both from within ourselves and watching some great comedians on television, was a great relief in our lives.

As I woke, the train went through a long tunnel and broke my thoughts. I wondered what the other interviewed girls from Darlington would look like. Young, old, serious, happy?. I looked around me at the passengers in my carriage. No sign of office types here, I thought.

Chapter One

Apparently there were to be seven of us. We were going to be trained at head office Hitchin, as motor insurance clerks.

Then we would be transferred back to Darlington, after three months, to open a new subsidiary office there. We girls, seven of us, became known as the Darlington Dollies.

Chapter 2

"Will you come to Bristol with me this weekend, Eileen?" I loved Tracy. She had dark brown, curly hair and was always smiling and happy. I suppose you would say she had a womanly body, with a cheeky wide mouth smile. Definitely number one Darlington dolly.

"Oh, well I could," I said. "How are you getting there?" It seemed she had friends at university there, and was going by coach to join the party scene for the weekend. Other closer friends within the Darlington dollies group had said no. I was pretty green but I agreed to go. Tracy was only a year older than me, but she was years ahead of me in being worldly wise. We laughed all the way to Bristol. I discovered I liked a coach journey. My father always had a car and all of our holidays had been by car or train, we sometimes slept an odd night in his car, if we were too late to find accommodation.

I loved Bristol and the people I met. We toured three or four pubs and Tracy was so chatty and happy with her friends. The only issue on that Saturday night was that I hadn't made a note of where we were staying, and when the group piled into a taxi, slightly drunk, I almost got left behind. I ran and banged on the taxi door, luckily he stopped and all was fine. We slept on her friend's sofas that night, and had some toast for breakfast, and then headed off to the coach station to return to Hitchin. I hadn't had much to drink on the pub crawl, so it was only Tracy who had a headache and slept for most of the coach journey home.

The other girls who made up our seven were all very nice. Two of them were very shy. Tracy was the ringleader and life and soul of our group. All six of them were placed in a large house called Elm Lodge, but I was housed separately with Mrs Chivers, in Milestone Road. "Mrs Chivers,- like the jelly" she said. I laughed. The company paid her my rent directly and then I received six pounds in wages per week. A huge increase to my circumstances.

However, before getting to Mrs. Chivers, I had to endure a very strange experience for two weeks at another employee's home. A married couple within the company answered the call for help to house one of us. Me! The couple seemed quite nice at first, the room was pleasant, though there were dolls of all kinds placed all over the house. They hardly spoke to me. At this point in my life I was very quiet myself. I was still sorting through the trauma in my mind of my home life, leaving the North, and getting used to a new job. One night I met all of the girls in the town center for a meal. Tracy had called to collect me and had been shown to my room. She was going to walk with me into town as she knew where the pub was. She was slightly freaked out by all of my landlady's dolls on display.

I had one glass of wine during the evening and walked home on my own. The house was in darkness when I got there. I quietly locked the door behind me and crept upstairs to bed. The next morning, the couple were pleasant over breakfast, and I left for work before the

Chapter Two

woman. At lunch time my boss asked to see me. They said the lady was claiming that I came in very late and had been sick in their bath. My God, this is serious! My mind buzzed with confusion. I could not take in that an older person than myself, would lie about me like this. All I could say was "it's not true." In my mind, thinking about it later, my boss must already have felt that this lady was not trustworthy, because it only took Tracy to step in and say that we had not been out late and that I had only had one drink. She also said that she thought they were an odd couple and described the dolls placed all over the house. I kept my job and was then placed with the lovely Mrs Chivers.

Chapter 3

My train pulled into Hitchin station and I was met by the lady of the couple who had interviewed me. She was driving their 1969 rather sporty Porsche. A car choice which surprised me, I think it was yellow. She and her husband were so quiet and studious, and so focused on work. Clearly they had a carefree side to them. The roads were a lot quieter in those days, and people definitely stared at them as they rode around the small market town. She took me to the office first, then introduced me to the lady whose home I would be staying at.

Later that evening I met my landlady's husband, also a quiet man. I was shy, but happy and full of excitement for my new situation. Just what did this quiet market town have in store for me?

Having settled in at work, the arduous task of understanding the insurance business began. I'd had a secondary school education, where after one year I was given the chance to move up to grammar school, but mum and dad couldn't agree about the move, so I decided to stay put. My school years were truly happy years for me. I made friends easily and the teachers were excellent.

Previously, at the age of eleven, just before taking the eleven plus exam, I'd lost my hearing. A bad cold affected both ears, sadly one eardrum was lost forever to an infection which took too long to clear.

It's astonishing how we cope. I had to watch people's mouths more, and rely totally on my better ear.

I never said at interviews that I had this problem, I just got on with it. I was once given the cane at school for ignoring the teacher, of course I hadn't meant to. I had some time off school when the infection and hearing loss first started, but I still managed to do well at the eleven plus exam. So instead of going to the local Council School, I made it into Leeholme Secondary Modern school. My mother was so excited that when she heard, she hugged me, lifting me into the air. My mum was not a hugger and it somewhat startled me, but still I felt a warm flush of happiness.

I became games captain, Head of house and eventually, in my last year, a prefect, wearing the badges proudly on my tie and blazer lapels.

In any event, this education enabled me to be a quick learner, and I soon got to grips with my new job.

I had taken a liking to one of the young men I worked with. He had dark brown hair, brown eyes, and a shy smile. One lunchtime as we rushed to grab a sandwich, I noticed him walking in front of me.

I cheekily reached forward and tugged at the bottom of his jacket. He turned and smiled back at me.

Later that day, he came over and leaned on my desk, and asked if I'd like to have a drink with him that evening. I flushed red and said that I would, and we agreed where to meet and when.

Chapter Three

I was nearer to 19 than 18 now, but I had next to no experience with men. The one date that I had when living at home, my father had stood at the front door, drawing on his cigarette, luckily we had returned in good time and I quickly went inside. I had at least been to a mixed school so I wasn't overly shy with the opposite sex.

In Hitchin, on our first date, we went to a local pub and had a pretty good evening where we chatted and made each other laugh. It seemed to go very well. It wasn't long before we were spending more time together at weekends. One of the other guys at work was a friend of his, and so we often spent time together, meeting up with even more friends that they knew. We travelled around the area to several little villages, to the popular pubs of the day. On another earlier date, we were sitting on a low level wall of a pub, when tyres screeched behind us, throwing up gravel in the car park. As I turned to look round, someone leapt over the top of our heads and landed on the concrete in front of us. I was astonished, he was identical to my date, in fact he was my date's twin. Graham had not told me about his twin Alan. I discovered he had an older brother too, but no sisters.

It was now the end of July and I had been in Hitchin for some seven or eight weeks. This small market town was so tranquil and full of so many diverse nationalities, and I was happy here. Such a change for me, it was very uplifting.

In those days I remember looking at the older generation walking around with panama hats, sunglasses, and smiling at everyone they met. For me, a northerner, I was more used to a flat cap being doffed, with similar gentle smiles but not so many sunglasses. Hitchin town center has lots of Tudor style buildings, which many tourists visited over the years. There was still a cattle market when I first arrived. It wasn't overly busy by this point, many farmers were suffering from the last foot and mouth outbreak in the mid sixties. It did however mean that the town was buzzing on a Saturday, with many rather happy people leaving the pubs, all the better for their afternoon drink.

I was so happy, Graham and Alan, my lovely twins, seemed to have a normal, busy, and to me, exciting life. Graham and his friend from work, Andrew, took me to the London Flying Club which was at Dunstable Downs, a picturesque place, where people pulled over from the road on top of the hill, to admire its beauty.

We drove on further, down the hill, and then indicated left into the grounds where there were hangers housing the gliders. After parking and visiting the office, Andrew got into a glider which was then winched into the sky. It was wonderful to watch him soar above our heads. How wonderful I thought. When he landed he glibly said, "I'll take Eileen up now."

It was unexpected, I think Graham had organised it, as I'm sure he would have loved to be in the air himself, but he was trying to impress me. They turned the glider back around and attached a fresh winch to the front. Andrew jumped into the front, I jumped into the seat behind him, the winch began pulling us. It was a little noisy as the underneath of the glider was dragged across the surface of the field leading to the cliff edge. As we took off, a wonderful elation came over me, -then the winch was released and after a small lurch, silence. Total silence! Andrew skillfully moved the glider in circular motions high in the sky, making the most of the thermals that day. The scenery was amazing from so high up. I looked to my left, over his head to the front, and then to my right. Fabulous! Sadly there weren't enough thermals for us to stay in the air for very long. Andrew turned the glider and aimed for our landing site. As we came down I felt incredibly nervous. I knew there were no wheels. The noise of graunching beneath us was quite alarming, but within seconds we had stopped and everything was ok. "Thank you so much Andrew," I said. "That was fantastic!"

It turned out that this was to be one of many exciting experiences that Graham and I would have with Andrew. He was a very skilled man. Only twenty two years of age, and he already had his pilot's license and had passed his sailing license too.

I'm not sure my company was very happy about Graham and I going out together. After all, they were investing large amounts of money into my training and I was supposed to go back to Darlington, to help open a brand new branch, which of course I did in fact do, when the three months training was up.

Mrs Chivers, however, loved to hear about my exploits with this amenable young man Graham. We often chatted over breakfast. One morning, just before breakfast, she came in from the front door laughing, and said "You'll never guess. I've had to send three young ladies away from the door. They think I've got Cilla Black staying with me." We did laugh. I suppose there was a similarity between Cilla and myself but I had mousy hair and she had red.

Most tv shows were shown in black and white only pictures in those days, so viewers wouldn't see her lovely red hair.

Mrs Chivers, I always called her that, (respect was very important in those days), was a small slim sixty something. She was a kind motherly lady with grey hair and glasses, who knew most of her neighbours, but she was also very savy and business like. I was happy telling her about my daily goings on, but I wouldn't call her a confidant. However, I do recall explaining to her how and why I had left home.

It was hard explaining the actual moment, without going into the years of mental torment leading to it, but emotionally I couldn't go there. I simply stated that there were lots of arguments between my parents. I told her about the note I left just before quietly going downstairs. I told her of the fear I felt as I leapt into the car. How my friends were happy for me as we drove to yet another friends' home, where they would take care of me for a few days until I looked for somewhere to live.

I told her of how short lived that happiness was, which then made me decide to leave the North of England for good.

I didn't relate to her why my happiness was short lived,-that within a few short hours of leaving home, there was heavy thumping on my friends front door. My friend, whose husband was a policeman, looked towards him, startled. He said "sit still I'll get it". It was my father, angry, and he was very insistent that I get myself out of there and come home. How did he know I was there?

I had forgotten that some weeks earlier he had given me a lift to a dress fitting there. One of the girls was great at sewing, and made me a rather nice dress for work.

The "policeman" husband stood his ground, he came back to me to say my mum was also there and would I speak with her. I loved my mum so much, I hated what my actions must be doing to her, but years of such a toxic life had taken its toll. They showed her in and she sat on the sofa across from me. She smiled kindly and pleaded with me to come back. She said things would change. In just a few short minutes I felt the urge to go back to my home. I so wanted to believe her.

As I fell silent and considered the situation, her face suddenly contorted and she snarled at me to get myself out of there and into the car. I knew at once I couldn't possibly go back with them. Who knew what would happen? I said "I'm sorry mum, I can't go back."

Chapter Three

Two or three days later my father actually came to where I worked. I came through the shop floor door into the reception and stopped in my pace, as if I'd hit a brick wall. Dad was sitting there in the reception area. Startled, I could only force myself to keep going and head for the main office door. He didn't want to see me, he didn't want to see my office manager, for some reason he wanted to see the works manager responsible for the men on the shop floor, who created the settees and chairs that we produced weekly. He apparently wanted to find out if I had a boyfriend and thought he could talk more easily with the male manager. My immediate manager was a lady, and her boss was also a woman.

After the men spoke together, dad left the building, and the tall kindly works manager came to see me.

He told me not to worry, he had explained that I was a quiet girl who worked well and was well thought of. He said that he had told my father there was nothing he could do to help change my decision. I was so grateful to this company, and the help they had given me, but I now knew that I needed to get out of the area altogether.

And so, as I relayed some of this story to Mrs Chivers, I realised that I had in fact achieved a lot in a very short time, even moving away from everything I knew.

During my three months of training, I only briefly met Graham's family. I worked hard, enjoyed my time with the girls, listened to their life stories, and saw Graham as often as possible. It was summer time and we spent weekends at the open air swimming pool, meeting friends, and some Saturday nights I watched Graham and his brothers sing and play folk music at the local pubs. They mainly played for the reward of a beer. I have to say they were really good.

The day to return to Darlington came slightly earlier for me than expected. The new office block was not quite finished. However, there was a temporary office on one floor within an old building in Darlington which the company was using whilst waiting for the new building. It was small and was being manned by three male staff. I presume because of my association with Graham, the company had decided to send me back early. They found me a one bedroomed flat, which was just across the road from this temporary office.

Chapter Four

Although I was sad to leave Graham. I was very happy to start my new position in Darlington. I had to get used to living on my own, there were no mobile phones in those days, so it wasn't easy to arrange meeting my old friends. I put into practice my training, taking motor insurance enquiry calls, and getting to know my workmates.

There were three of us in our small office. One chap was very anti my arrival. He seemed to hate me. He even said my surname of Marshall made me sound as if I was of black descent. Blimey, he wouldn't get away with that today!

I was fortunate that my elder brother and sister-in-law had kept in touch, I was able to have dinner with them on the weekends. I did a bit of babysitting for them. They lived in a small village in a newly built home fifteen minutes from Darlington. Crazily, two managers from my company bought their home on the exact same estate, in preparation of their move from Hitchin to Darlington with the company. They eventually became friends with my brother and his wife.

Luckily for me, the new office block became ready for us to move into.

I found that I was back with my Darlington dollies, all in the same, rather large, open plan office. Of course it would never be the same as in Hitchin, Tracy now had her own friends that she came back to, and two of our girls, the shy ones, didn't return to Darlington. So much for sending me back early, it turned out I wasn't the one to worry about.

So I had arrived in Hitchin in June of 1969, and returned to Darlington by September and we were now settling in and heading for Christmas.

Since my arrival back in Darlington Graham sent me several love letters. I wrote to him too and occasionally, he phoned me at work and we were able to have a few quiet words. I was missing Graham and I knew I was certainly missing Hitchin. When Graham suggested that I come and spend Christmas with him and his family for our week's break, I felt rather excited about it. We had been three months apart, much more time than we had spent together. However, my wage was now more in line with working up North and once again I had to pay my own rent. So I hadn't saved enough money to travel back to Hitchin. Graham immediately said he would send me a ticket.

I felt so spoilt and needed, and didn't hesitate to agree. When I reached Hitchin for a second time, Graham was there smiling and happy to see me. My tummy had butterflies, I was falling in love and was missing him more than I had realised.

We had a lovely festive time together, his parents home and the spare room were lovely. I took to Graham's parents very well.

His mother had beautiful, bright, smiling, hazel eyes, and a rather large bouffant hairstyle, I think to make up for her small stature. His brothers were full of fun and very talented.

Graham, Alan, (his twin), and his elder brother Richard, all played the guitar and sang, mainly folk music. The older brother was

Chapter Four

particularly good on various instruments. Alan was amazing on banjo, I always loved watching him play, his fingers covered in metal picks, moving so fast as he plucked the strings.

When I met their father, I thought he was a kindly, and perhaps shy man. He was over six foot tall with grey hair and he enjoyed smoking menthol cigarettes. I later found out that he was a fisherman and a director of the family business. I hardly saw much of him as most of his spare time was spent on the banks of various rivers around the country. He was a prolific writer of fishing articles and fishing books.

Graham and I had a wonderful few days, Christmas was full of laughter, and visiting the local pubs. His twin brother seemed to get a kick out of teasing me, they were all so easy to get on with.

It was sad leaving Hitchin again, Graham looked forlorn, I felt so many emotions. It had been so good and yet I had another life to return to.

My mum told me lots of stories as I was growing up. Apparently in 1919 dad had lost both parents at the age of only two, in a car accident. Cars were slower then but much heavier and more dangerous. He was born in Nuneaton, but was brought up by an aunt in Birmingham. For years I called her nan, and thought my uncle was dad's brother. It turned out he was dad's cousin. Dad was in the army during WW2, I'm not sure if he joined because of the war or was already joined. He had looked after prisoners of war towards the end, had fought at Dunkirk, and met my mum whilst stationed at Catterick Camp. I often used to ponder whether the hell of Dunkirk or his orphaned life was the reason for his violent outbursts.

I remember there were also many happy times of laughter and treats with dad, my sister and younger brother thought the world of him. For a start, by the time my younger brother was born dad had slowed down somewhat. My sister was already at school on the day mum was beaten. So they didn't have my memory and didn't go through that particular hell.

We travelled all over the UK in dad's little car, he loved driving, he made sure we had a holiday somewhere every year. If we passed a broken down car, he would roll up his sleeves and sort the problem out for the people. He was a whizz with anything mechanical, army training I expect. My mum would sigh, knowing we would lose an hour or so helping them out.

I recall he took my elder brother to Scotland, they went on their own, climbing the hills and thoroughly enjoying the scenery and fresh air. They bought us all lovely gifts, I think I got a pen set, probably the same for my sister. We visited Devon and Cornwall, London, the Lake District, Blackpool, Whitby, Redcar, Newcastle and the list goes on. His car was his pride and joy and enabled many, many family holidays.

My mum lived in a small village called West Auckland whilst she was growing up. She was the eldest child and went into service at a grand house when she finished school. She was used to nice clothes and often made her own hats to compliment them. I thought my mum was so pretty with light blue eyes and black hair mostly styled into a page boy look.

Her mum, my grandmother, was a large lady who always pulled her hair up into a severe bun. She also had bright, light blue eyes, but had full cheeks and a small mouth.

I don't remember my maternal Irish grandfather but by all accounts, he was a kind man. He fought in World War one, had 6 children and endured the 1930s depression, there was 70% unemployment in the

North East at that time. My mother talked about him often and he seemed of a quiet but strong character. He certainly did all he had to do to look after his family, proudly, and fairly.

Mum said, he once banged on the handle of my pram saying "ah you shitty arsed little beggar you". I'm glad she told me as it is my only connection with him. Not a memory, but a picture conjured up by my mum's memory. He died when I was only one year old.

My grandmother became the breadwinner then.

There were stories of granddad being a poacher, with a small poachers gun hidden in his coat. Apparently rabbit was often provided for the weekly meal.

I recall my mum saying that her mum once sold sweets from her living room, to generate an income.

When as a teenager, I visited nan with my mum, I began to realise that nan had turned her living room into a storage room for a business. It was always cluttered with clothes, lamps, and gadgets. Mum said nan would buy whatever people were getting rid of, then resell the item at a profit. It seems people came to her when they needed money, bringing with them an item to barter with. She also loaned money, charging interest, and collecting the debt weekly from the person. I had to conclude that my nan was a back street money lender. Gosh!

Chapter Five

Now back in Darlington after a truly happy Christmas, I got on with the task of doing my job and going out with friends again. Several times the girls and I went to the Gretna Green Wedding Inn on the edge of Newton Aycliffe. They did a folk song night once a week and it was a great night out.

I remember having a night out in Darlington itself, I can't remember which pub it was, but I do remember we all had to leave quickly, when suddenly the metal railings around the drinks and glasses at the bar were pulled down, police with dogs had entered and from our position one floor up, we made the decision to leave. I can only assume it was a drug bust, or some such thing.

Graham and I were still sending letters to each other. He was now openly asking me to come back. He felt sure I would land a job and he said he had talked with his mum and dad, and they were willing to house me. Graham had a full and interesting life, he had most of his family around him. Whereas I only saw my older brother at this point.

It made more sense for me to be the one to move. My sister, always difficult, had been very cool towards me, and my younger brother was still only about twelve.

I had spoken with my father on the telephone. He rang me once or twice at work but we were still estranged. I was less fearful now, as I was no longer trapped, and he seemed now to accept the situation. Dad had also suffered a heart attack at the time when I was with my first landlady in Newton Aycliffe, my elder brother had collected me and taken me to the hospital to see him. I was glad dad made progress, though I doubted he would give up smoking or alter his diet. I myself had now taken up the smoking habit, soon after coming back from my training in Hitchin. I could only afford a pack of ten cigarettes every few days, so I was not a big smoker at that point.

I think it was at the end of February 1970, - that I made the decision to quit my job and return to Graham. I was very nervous about having to live with his parents, looking back, it was extremely generous of them. This time I booked a cheaper coach ticket for my journey, -I would arrive in a small town called Baldock. This lovely little town had lots of coaching inns as it had been one of the main stopping points for actual horse driven coaches many years previously. Graham's mum and he came to pick me up. We were all excited and happy, though it must have seemed strange for Alan. Graham and Alan had a large bedroom with twin beds, the walls had tribal shields and an animal head as decor. There were lots of books. Clearly this was a bachelor existence, at the time now aged 19, I don't think I realised what an upheaval this would be for the twins. The elder brother was already married, and was renting a flat with his new wife, on the edge of Hitchin.

Chapter Five

The bedroom I had also had twin beds, and their maternal grandma and I shared the room at one point. She always came to stay with her daughter for a few weeks, once or twice a year. A lady of small stature like Graham's mum, she was silver haired, had an amazing memory, recited many long poems to us, and had an ability to touch her toes without bending her knees. She had a lovely sense of humor, I really took to her.

Fortunately, I found a job almost at once. This time it was at a life assurance company where I would become part of a team of six people, within again, an open plan office.

I made a good friendship with my team leader, a friendship which lasted for over forty years. My life moved so fast. Graham wanted to marry, we set a date for eight month's time. My soon to be sister-in-law agreed to make my wedding dress, she also loaned me her lovely long veil from her own wedding. We were able to secure rental accommodation on the same estate as her and Richard. Graham's parents said we could marry at the church in the next street from us, their regular, and have the reception in their garden. It was all moving along so fast. I made the decision to go home to see my parents. To spend a day or two, to explain how life had developed and to show them my engagement ring.

I was pretty on edge, but I wanted to do the right thing. My dad had made occasional phone calls to me, always keeping in touch. It was hard to talk, we were never able to clear the air, I think he wanted to assure my mum that I was ok. Their fights continued on, maybe more verbal than before, my younger brother taking the brunt of it now. My parents took my news well, and apart from my father finding my engagement ring and quietly hiding it from me, all went well. I had washed my hands and forgotten to put the ring back on, after a short while I realised, and went back to the bathroom, but it had gone. After seeing me get upset, dad then passed it back to me telling me to be more careful.

Graham and I managed another visit to my parents, before the wedding day. We travelled by coach, my elder brother had us stay with him, and dad met us in a pub.

So Graham and I did all we could to form a relationship with my mum and dad, but my parents still turned down their wedding invitation.

The day of the wedding was wonderful. Glenda, my soon to be sister-in-law, looked great in her bridesmaid outfit, wearing her long hair up, and threading a pink ribbon through the curls. Her dress echoed my own, but was in a pink cotton with flower print. Mine was a thick satin, as it was an autumn wedding. It had a slight puff to the sleeve which tapered down to my wrists. Both dresses were long to the top of our shoes. My dress was truly perfect to me. Graham's parents looked very smart.

Graham and I were very nervous, after all, we were both only nineteen and twenty years old, he was older than me by eight months.

My elder brother gave me away, all of Graham's family came, I had some friends from work, and my sister and sister-in-law, plus my three nephews, came too. Graham's formidable, paternal grandmother also came and it was a happy time at the reception. Finally, we changed our clothes and sped off in a taxi to start our honeymoon.

During those first years, before the children filled our lives, we experienced so many things.

Chapter Five

One friend loved motor racing and we went to Silverstone several times, to see many of the old classic cars speeding round the track. We could also wander around the pits freely in those days.

One night we went lamping. Charging around the farmer's field, guns ready. When the lamp at the front of our land rover was turned on, it mesmerised the poor hare, who was then cleanly shot. I only went once.

Andrew arranged to take his new girlfriend Sheila, with Graham and I on a rented yacht. Our summer holiday that year. I was so excited. Sheila was a lovely girl, who is still a dear friend to this day.

We set off in one car and headed off to Ramsgate. The first problem happened as we drove along the motorway. Something snapped on the front wheels. Somehow Andrew managed to steer the car up onto the approaching slip road, without causing an accident. We were so lucky the slip road was there. After a fair wait, our car was towed away and a provided courtesy car got us on our way again.

The yacht was a six berth twin keel, and looked lovely. The weather was blustery and the sea looked somewhat wild. When we checked the yacht over, as we put our baggage and provisions below, it transpired none of the four life jackets provided were functional. There should have been six in any case. Andrew asked if we could all swim, I said I couldn't. "Ok. We will tie a rope on you when needed" he said.

Young and foolish, none of us were at all phased by this.

Andrew and his very amateur crew set sail, it was a force seven. Within minutes I was gushing with delight, riding the waves with my legs balancing me up and down, - high on adrenaline.

Andrew shouted, "Are you ok Graham?" I turned and saw that Graham had turned a dreadful green colour. Andrew was already maneuvering us back towards shore. Poor Graham, I had been so excited, I had not noticed that he had become ill. We spent another night in England, waiting for better weather.

The next morning the weather had improved significantly. Graham was well again, and we set off once more. After a little while, Andrew was able to set the sails and turn the engine off, and we began tacking our way to France.

I was truly loving this experience. It didn't matter that a huge thick rope was tied around my waist because I couldn't swim. I ran my fingers through the tops of the waves, I breathed in more deeply than usual, I reveled in the wind blowing through my hair.

Sheila was chatting to Andrew, they both pulled on their cigarettes, he was rushing around now and again to adjust a sail, both of them bobbing under the boom as it changed sides.

In the afternoon, Graham was pretty tired, we'd had some red wine with our lunch and it was mingling with the wonderful, salty, sea air making him sleepy.

I too was relaxing, letting the sun and breeze envelope my bare legs and arms.

Graham decided to climb into the little dinghy which we were trailing. He put the oars on one side of himself, and put his arms up and his hands under his head. Soon he was sleeping peacefully, the little dinghy rocking him gently as we tacked along.

It was about half an hour later that Graham shouted "oh hell, I've lost the oars". We all turned and looked at him, then the dinghy, then at the surface of the ocean, scanning the area around him. "You bloody plonker Graham" Andrew exclaimed. We pulled on the rope which attached the dinghy to our yacht, drawing him closer, and helping him to step back on board.

Chapter Five

I have to say we kind of just moved on and accepted the loss. Andrew was looking at the map and a decision was made that we would enter the estuary into the port of Gravelines.

As we travelled into the safety of the harbour, several figures along the sides were waving at us and shouting. I'm afraid we couldn't understand what they were saying.

Andrew waved back, and we made our way as far in as we could. He tried to make contact with the harbourmaster via radio, and when that failed he tried sounding "Q" on the horn. We had no luck so we dropped anchor and Andrew and Graham decided to use the dinghy to row in and find the guy.

"Ah! No oars" said Graham.

Never one to be phased, Andrew grabbed a saucepan and the frying pan. "These will do." he said.

Somewhere in my treasure boxes, to this day, some fifty years later, I have a picture of the two of them "rowing" towards the steps with a pan and frying pan flashing in and out of the water.

Anyway, they were soon back with our passports and it seems we were of no real interest to those in charge. A little later we all "rowed" back to land together, in the hope of finding a cafe.

We soon found one nearby, my memory is now vague but I recall how friendly the people were. How happy we all were, and that we took the man's business card at his insistence. It's as well we had a few drinks, because we were about to find out why the locals had been waving and shouting at us when we first arrived.

The sea had disappeared. Our yacht, though upright, was surrounded by mud. Had our yacht been single keel it would have fallen over onto its side. The dinghy would now be useless to us. Fresh on happiness and drink, we took off our shoes and slowly plodded through the sticky mud, until we reached the yacht. I'm not sure how we managed to clean ourselves up, but as young, foolish, idiots, it was a great adventure which has made me laugh many times over the years.

So we had a few lovely days, sailing, stopping here and there to enjoy the local food, and practicing our culinary skills. I loved sailing, it was a holiday I never forgot. Sadly the day before we were due home, the weather turned. Andrew said we couldn't sail home or even just use the engine. We had to be home for work on Monday, so it was decided that three of us would get a ferry home, and poor Andrew would sail the boat back to England on his own as soon as the weather improved. Oh dear.

The ferry home was of course safer but the roll of the ferry was very bad and it made our last few hours on holiday a bit of a nightmare.

Those early days of marriage were full of fun and hectic goings on.

We both worked hard, but at weekends lots of Graham's friends would call in. We lived yards from his elder brother, and often his mum would invite us over for dinner. Alan had been dating a lovely local girl called Janet for some months. Neither of the twins could drive at this point, but Janet could, and was often picking Alan up in her little mini, heading off on a date somewhere. My mum-in-law loved her and of course Graham and I had moved out into our own rented place. So happily, his mum saw more of them at this point. It is only now, many years later that I realise how empty the house must have begun to feel for her. Her older boy had already moved, and now Graham, but luckily she worked part time as an auxiliary nurse. She had long time friends in the street, and a loving family and her own mum was still alive and living with one of her sisters.

Chapter Six

Not quite four months on from our wedding day, Graham's mother sadly died. It was a devastating time for Graham and his family.

Graham was still only twenty years old and he was greatly affected by his mum's passing. In just under two months time it would be his twenty first birthday. So sad.

That year so much was going on, Alan and Janet married and continued living at the family home for a while, my sister was being dated by Graham's best man. They had met at our wedding and Jim had been very keen on her. He had to go up and down the motorway to the little village where I once lived, and then eventually, she took the same path as myself and moved South to Hitchin.

I often reflected that it was so good that Janet and Alan first lived at the family home after they married. It meant that we could all still go there for quite a while, which helped immensely with handling the loss. Eventually though, their father decided to sell the family home and there was a point in time when all three of the brothers and wives lived on the same estate, renting, prior to buying their own homes over time.

Janet and Alan were the first to start a family, and a beautiful boy called Iaan entered our lives. I loved holding him, feeding him his bottle, making him laugh as the months passed and he took more interest in the world. Janet was an excellent mother, I was amazed at how quickly he absorbed the world around him and learned. I was seven when my baby brother was born, and I was already at school so I don't recall much of him as a new baby. I do remember mum letting his blonde, curly hair grow and grow until it was way past his shoulders, reaching down his back. I don't think she wanted to lose the baby stage with him.

Janet was the same with her two boys, she had her second baby the same year that I had my first. I seem to recall that both of her boys grew their hair very long, with curls cascading down their back.

Graham seemed restless, he had worked in Luton after leaving his Hitchin job. Then he changed his job again. My mum came to stay with us at a point when she was very poorly. We had a small hospital in Hitchin at that time and it was easier for me to get help for my mum. She had terrible problems with her lungs. Years of smoking unfiltered Woodbines had damaged her lungs. They did lots of tests and gave her an inhaler which helped greatly.

Work, caring for mum and her hospital visits, plus Graham not settling wherever he worked made life stressful. I thought the loss of his mother must have badly affected him, more than I realised. Gradually my mum improved and returned to dad, then Graham decided to go for a job he had seen in the Suffolk area. His dad tried to dissuade him, but by now we were both looking for a change, something to turn our lives around. Graham was lying about things, I didn't know what to think. His brothers seemed exasperated with him. I stood firmly with him and said I was excited by this new start with his new

Chapter Six

job. He had passed his driving test and had been driving an oldish car for about a year now. The job came with a new car which pleased him.

Essentially he became a salesman, selling life assurance and accident protection policies. He was given a car and earned commission on his sales.

We spent a few weekends viewing the area and looking for our first house to purchase.

In those days buying a house was a much easier process. It wasn't long before we were ready to move and for Graham to start his new job.

We drove off from Hitchin on a sunny day, unloaded our furniture in warm sunshine, and took pictures of our lovely end of terrace home on a street in Ipswich, Suffolk.

Graham seemed renewed, he quickly painted out the adjoining office/small bedroom leading off our main bedroom. He seemed to love his work, and we soon made friends with two couples on the street. I had been successful at a job interview for counter staff at the Ipswich and Suffolk building society. The people there were lovely, and some months in, my boss discovered that his favourite fisherman, and author of some excellent fishing books, was my father-in-law. This led to him corresponding with my father-in-law and he was truly overjoyed to get a response.

I was able to start up a netball team for the building society, we weren't very good, but it was good fun. We played against other companies and also the fire brigade staff once. However, the husbands and boyfriends of our team of ladies became restless when we were not successful, it kind of took the edge off it.

I was happy and I thought Graham was too, but I was being lied to. He was failing once again at work, but not telling me.

We had his lovely maternal grandmother come to stay with us for two weeks. His aunt, so like his mum in attitude, was a loving, caring presence. She missed her sister's help in having the grandmother to stay, giving her a much needed rest. I said we had room and could have her, but it was a long journey to reach us now, as they lived in Ware. She was so grateful and happy, and "little nan" soon settled in with us for a two week holiday. Such a fit lady in some ways, she prepared the vegetables for our evening meal whilst we were at work. Graham was so lucky to have such a loving family, yet he seemed distant from them to my mind. I seemed to take the lead in organising visits or get-togethers.

I think nan enjoyed her stay and it was lovely to have family around when they came to take her home.

Two years on and we were now expecting our first child, it should have been a wonderful period for us, but I realised that whilst I was at work, he was keeping our female next door neighbour company and not working. She was a stay at home mum.

My parents travelled down to visit us after I opened up about my concerns. I seem to remember being very upset, hormones and anger I assume. Actually, this was very good of my parents because it was a long trip, and neither of them were in good health. They found that they couldn't help in any way because Graham simply pretended to work from home and shut himself in the office.

It was nevertheless a good visit, mum was coping fairly well with her asthma and seemed not too bad mentally.

A few months later when I was around six months pregnant, Graham said we needed to move to reduce outgoings, especially as I would soon be off work for a few months.

Chapter Six

We were able once again to sell and buy quickly. Now we were settled in Stowmarket, a small market town outside of Ipswich. Thankfully, away from the overly friendly neighbour.

A month later our lovely daughter Samantha was born. In those days you were in hospital for about a week, resting, learning to feed and care for your baby. My sister and her husband Jim, (Graham's best man at our wedding), came to see the baby. They had married each other about a year after our wedding.

When Graham picked Samantha and myself up from the hospital, I was really disappointed at the state of the house. He hadn't even connected the heating properly to warm the upstairs rooms. I soon got it sorted but I was fast becoming a fixer instead of a happy new mother and wife.

I loved being a mother, Samantha was a delight, her hair was almost silver and she had light green eyes which I found fascinating. I think her eyes came from Graham's rather formidable paternal grandmother. A short stout lady with a huge personality. Samantha's nature was jovial, inquisitive, and very alert. It was always difficult to settle her, as the slightest noise brought her back to wakefulness.

We took Samantha at two months old to see my mum and dad. Poor mum was clearly suffering from dementia and some kind of muscle problem. I was glad we made the effort, as only two and a half months later, dad had another heart attack and died. My younger brother and dad had been caring for mum, and this can't have helped with his own health condition.

My elder brother took over managing the funeral and the family financial affairs. I was in a bit of a daze, it was hard to have such a young baby and be of any use. I had returned to the building society part time, I knew Graham was not doing well with his job, we were missing my full time wages .

My elder brother took mum into his home as my younger brother was still only just eighteen years old.

He and his wife were doing their best to get mum into a care home but she was still only fifty nine, a bit young to qualify for a place.

After dad's funeral Graham and I took mum for a month, then after another brief spell with my brother, she went into a care home at West Auckland, her hometown, where I too had lived my first two years of life. It was so sad but it was the right thing to do for mum.

Within just a couple of months I was sitting in our bank, where we had our mortgage, Samantha on my knee. I was pleading for time to pay apparent arrears. Graham had been hiding the post and so this was quite a shock to me. He just wasn't making enough sales and was getting very little commission. I was successful in holding the bank off and Graham's father provided money for us to pay the arrears. We gave a promise to repay him.

I took a cheque to the building society a week after my first meeting there, but sadly within two days, Graham had withdrawn his dad's money and spent it on goodness knows what.

The building society sent us an eviction letter. Graham's parents and I were in disbelief. He never gave them a good explanation as far as I know as to how he had spent the money, and he just stayed completely silent when I tried to talk to him to find out what had happened. We had to leave. We lost our home. Thankfully, Alan and Janet took us in. We were back in Hitchin.

Chapter Seven

The first time I met nan, Graham's paternal grandmother, was also the first Christmas that I spent with Graham and his family. She lived in the nearby town of Letchworth.

We pulled through open gates and parked in front of an amazing house.

It was clearly old, with worn looking bricks and had tall tudor style chimneys. The windows were diamond leaded glass and the wooden door, which creaked as it slowly opened, was made of heavy oak in Tudor style. To the side of the door was a bell that you had to reach up to and move the chain to make it clang.

As we chatted, in Christmas spirit, presents in hand, we heard footsteps slowly cross the large entrance hall. A large clunk was heard as the bolt moved from within the frame, a squeaky loud click released the latch and the door swung open. A well rounded, medium framed woman of around sixty plus years, was greeting us all. "Come in, come in". I noted an accent which turned out to be Austrian. This was Elsa, Nan's companion of the last twenty or so years.

Graham's mum greeted her warmly, the twins giving a quick kiss to her cheek. I took in the scene behind her as she leaned forward. A huge minstrel gallery framing the upper part of the hallway, with dark wooden stairs cutting down to the left of the hall, before straightening out towards us. She led us across a black and white tiled floor, covered here and there with persian type rugs, into the living room. It was quite a dark room, despite the lights being on.

The whole room had dark panel walls and to one side of the huge wooden fireplace sat nan, the reflection of the twinkling flames of the fire dancing on her face. She filled the large wing chair, her legs stretching the fabric of her skirt, her arms each resting importantly on the side supports. She looked towards us, her coloured, light brown hair framing her rather amply cheeked face.

We all found a seat and Nan's booming strong voice filled the room. She regaled us with stories of work and past adventures, she was about seventy I think, and she was still going into her office daily. She had interesting and humorous stories of her past life, and it was apparent that she did not suffer fools and had a snarky side to her character. Like many old people of that time, she could recite poems, some extremely long ones, and she never forgot a single word or line. After cups of tea and a slice of one of Elsa's home made cakes, it was time to leave.

Once back in the car, it was clear that visiting nan was a mixed pleasure for the family. I think they loved the old house, the guys remembered hiding in the priest hole in the living room when they were boys. As young kids it was very exciting. But nan was an overpowering person and they clearly felt sorry occasionally for Elsa, who took the brunt of nan's moods. Being a daughter-in-law can't have been much fun for Graham's mum.

Chapter Seven

The old lady and I seemed to hit it off quite well. She had a knack of making you feel that she liked you.

Nan had her family, but she also had many friends, gathered over the years, and also a large amount of work "friends". She had a habit of treating her business customers as long lost friends. She showed concern and compassion for any family loss or problems. I think she did genuinely feel for them, but it was also a good strategy for many years of continued business with them. Because of her many personal friends, and many business connections, her actual family had to always, "phone first" when planning a weekend visit to see her. If you didn't check, you could easily end up with Elsa firmly explaining that nan was having tea with A or B, and that you should phone later and organise another day.

Through the week, her son would drive to her home in the mornings. Nan, always in a coloured woolen suit with accessorised jumper, would walk with her stick to his car and get in, to be driven to work. Once there they would park at the back of the factory, in order to avoid the concrete stairs leading from the footpath up to the front lawn in front of the offices. Nan would then say "good morning" to each and every employee that she passed, weight on stick, making her way through to her office.

This dear lady had a very full and active life. Her only son became a famous fisherman and worked with her in the family owned business, manufacturing lawnmowers. Many famous golf courses used her mowers around the world. Many racecourses were cut by the chain link gang mowers which they produced. She was very proud of her achievements. On the queen's silver jubilee, she had a normal lawnmower fitted out in stainless steel, rather than painted, to be gifted to the queen. Then, she of course made sure that the local papers ran a story about it.

She wrote a cookery book and using her son's publisher got it published, mainly to prove that when she was younger she could indeed cook well. Elsa, you see, was now doing the cooking. When nan entertained, it was Elsa who got praise for her skills and culinary delights! I think it irked nan over time.

This cookery book led to nan appearing on the Russell Harty show. I still possess the DVD which one of her employees made of the show. In my opinion, Russell did take the mickey out of her a little, by producing from Harrods a squirrel stew. He got the audience to taste it, then asked Nan to tell them what they were eating. She and her son had travelled to London, carrying a specially cooked trout on their knees, only to have the squirrel stew presented instead. Hilarious, but Nan was not amused.

Chapter Eight

During our stay with Janet and Alan, Graham was still behaving badly. He was lying to his employers about meetings with potential customers, eventually getting the sack. I can't remember how long he was unemployed for now, but I recall after a couple of months of staying with his brother, we managed to rent a maisonette back on the estate where we had once all lived. He had to travel to Luton now for work.

I found a job in Hitchin itself and sorted out a lovely lady to look after our daughter. I saw my old friends again, though Graham seemed to move on to a new set. His new set of friends were married, one of them was actually married to a girl I once worked with. The other couple were newly married,

Graham had met them down at the pub.

Of course, once again he had to muddy the waters. I was working part time and caring for Samantha. When I did get to go out in the evening and meet up with his friends, I was pretty sure he was messing with the new wife.

We of course rowed about this, but he assured me that I was wrong. It was some years later that I found out he had indeed had an affair and ruined their marriage.

It wasn't until I was expecting and only a month away from giving birth to our son, that I finally knew for sure that Graham was having yet another affair. I was on maternity leave now and had had a couple of telephone calls from a woman. Each time claiming a wrong number, the last time saying he was her boyfriend.

At eight months pregnant I knew there was little I could do. I resolved to ask him to leave once the baby was born. We of course argued which was not good for anyone.

One morning whilst Graham was at work, there was a loud insistent banging of the front door. I waddled down the stairs of the maisonette to answer the door. Several men stood before me. I was shown a card, they were plain clothed policemen.

I sat down on the stairs as they pushed past me and began searching the whole house.

One guy, the one who showed me the card, was telling me they had had an anonymous phone call tipping them off about Graham having ammunition. I could hear them entering the loft area now.

"Can I phone my husband?" I asked.

"Do you know if he has ammunition?"

"Yes, but it's old stuff and not live." I said. Graham and his twin had always collected war memorabilia. I took no real notice of it, as it held no interest for me.

I told them that the ammunition was in a cartridge box in the hall cupboard where my hoover was. They pulled it out and checked it over. They could see it was all collectors items but they said they would still have to take it and have it checked out. I complained that they were out of order, forcibly going through all of our cupboards

Chapter Eight

and scaring an eight month pregnant woman. The tall rather severe man in charge simply stated that I was lucky they had not broken in my door and pointed guns at me. Bloody hell!!

It seems that Graham had riled a work colleague. The man was so pissed off that he decided to use his knowledge of Graham's collection to get him into trouble.

Graham managed to persuade the police not to detonate his collection. He got them to send it up to Cambridge and get it specially x-rayed. I didn't fully understand it all, but essentially they could see all the pieces were empty and were only to be used for collector resale.

He got his collection back.

The night before our son James was born, we had a huge fight about his present girlfriend. I cried so much and couldn't sleep. Then at 6am I had a dreadful back ache. This was it. I don't get contractions before my waters break, well if I do I don't feel them. So bearing in mind my first pregnancy, where the hospital had sent me home once, and then two weeks later, poor Samantha was almost too long in the womb, I had to get to hospital quickly. Graham got up and took me in. An hour and a half later James was born, a headful of black hair, a red distorted face and brown eyes coming towards me as they laid him on me. Graham was surprisingly happy, he had a boy, - despite all my pain and misery I noted his reaction. He had loved his daughter too, at her moment of birth, but he seemed incapable of being a father and husband.

This time I was only in the hospital for three or four days. Our rental maisonette was more modern than the house we had in Stowmarket, so we had underfloor electric heating. A better homecoming for our second baby. Graham had to look after Samantha whilst I was in the hospital, she was going to be three in a couple of days time. I managed to make a birthday cake and relied on Graham to sort presents for Samantha.

A week after this Graham informed me he would be moving out of our home and would be moving in with his present girlfriend.

I was a bit numb really, I knew of the affair, I knew we would probably part, but I was nursing James, I had no idea how I would support myself and two children. Having adjusted to the move back to Hitchin, and seeing Graham hold on to a job, (he was apparently happy again), especially with his own family around him, we wanted to have a second child to complete our family.

We both wanted a boy, and we were so lucky that James fulfilled our wishes. I would never want to be without either of my lovely children, but it seems I was wrong to have trusted Graham.

He did move out, his elder brother was furious with him. He went to see Graham, he looked through the window of his new home before knocking on the door. He could see Graham with his feet up on a stool, laying back reading, with a tiny kitten on his lap. He told me this made him so angry, his brother looking without a care in the world, whilst I attended to a crying young baby and an upset three year old.

After three or four weeks, the girl he moved in with crumbled from the pressure of splitting our family, and he came back home. Financially I had no choice but to let him back in. Soon I was back to work, but we couldn't move past the issues. Graham went to spend a few days with his friend Andrew who was now married to Sheila and who now had children of their own.

As they were mainly his friends, I wasn't able to talk in depth with them myself, but long after Graham and I split for good, they

Chapter Eight

remained friends with me and ultimately told me of his stay with them. He didn't say much to them except that his present life was not for him. He even stole from them whilst on that short break. Andrew's dictaphone fell out of Graham's jacket pocket, when Sheila moved it from a chair. Sheila got angry with him after just a few days, saying he should be with his family, looking after us. He came home.

Of course the marriage was doomed, we battled on until James was about two years old and inevitably another woman arrived on the scene. A divorced lady with children of her own.

After he left for good, the children and I spent two or three more years in Hitchin, but I had already decided to move to Letchworth. I checked out the schools first and then went to the council offices. I had only ever lived in either privately owned homes or rental property, but Graham's cheques constantly bounced, my part time wages couldn't cope with the outgoings. We were living in an upstairs maisonette since leaving Janet and Alan, underground electric heating was expensive.

I put emphasis on my children's health and after a couple of years we were offered a terraced home.

Shortly after settling into our home in Letchworth , I gave up smoking and used the money I was saving to take one driving lesson a week.

Fifteen weeks later I passed my test. At that time I had a lovely friend whom I met at one of my work places. She also lived on her own with two lovely girls, she was such a good mother.

Astonishingly, when she heard that I'd passed my test, 1984 I think, she offered me her car which she was upgrading. You could only drive about thirty miles before the oil light came on, other than that it was great. Wow! She said she would accept £300 and that I could pay her

£30 a month until it was paid for. What a wonderful lady. I continued saving money by not smoking in order to pay my friend for the car.

The car meant I could get a better job, I could take the children more often to visit their grandparents, shopping would be so much easier.

I had taken to riding a bicycle after Graham left. I had a child seat on the back. Often whilst Samantha was at school, James and I would whizz along the Hitchin streets to the shops in town, and we would return with James on the back and two full shopping bags, one balanced on each handlebar.

I was about thirty years old then and probably at my fittest ever with this bike. I remember going from Hitchin, up the hill to Letchworth, to visit the children's great grandma with James.

Once I was a bit too confident. Our dog Max darted through a gap in the hedge at King George's park in Hitchin. I followed him at speed, but one of the pedals of my bike caught the fence post hidden within the hedge.

We came to an abrupt stop. I somehow managed not to go over the handlebars, but we landed on our side. James was unhurt and stood up first, Max came back to check we were ok, I was confused for a short while but we were unhurt and that was the main thing.

How life changes. I'd had eighteen years of sometimes happy, sometimes traumatised life.

Now I had a second life with freedom, marriage, and motherhood. I resolved to make sure the children would know, love, and enjoy their family despite their father leaving.

Chapter Nine

For most of my life, I have always been optimistic, happy and I think helpful to others. Meeting Graham and his wonderful family was one of the best things to happen to me, but I was duped by Graham himself.

They were indeed all lovely people, but Graham was a problem. Now he was my problem!! We agreed for him to pay me around three hundred pounds a month. I worked part time, and my sisters-in-law were great. They still supported me with childminding and visits. My children always knew and played with their cousins.

To support myself in doing my part time job, I had a registered childminder and I used a day nursery too.

Poor Samantha had developed asthma shortly after we returned to Hitchin, and James had terrible eczema at four months old.

I recall that most nights I lost sleep during those early years. James was in terrible distress most nights, I had special cream for him, it was mainly his arms and legs that were problematic. I used to put cotton socks over all of his limbs and tape them to him in an attempt to stop him scratching. Samantha would also be woken by his crying. At least once or twice in the week Samantha would wake with asthma. She had different inhalers and sometimes we were able to borrow the surgery's nebuliser to get her through a bad bout. Nowadays these machines are readily available for patients to buy.

At least twice a year the doctor came out and slowly fed adrenaline into her vein. She hated that and it broke my heart. Her tiny pyjama covered frame, flushed red face, and tearful eyes, as she gasped for breath, tore at my senses. But although it took a good five minutes to slowly get adrenaline into her, it worked.

I used to call those years my "hammer house of horror" years.

James found it difficult to concentrate at school, he was always scratching his wrists on rough surfaces to gain relief from the itchiness. Eventually the doctor prescribed Vallergan, to numb the feeling, and of course the side effect was sleepiness.

His headmistress, a wonderful Welsh lady, took on an extra classroom assistant, just for James. She said that provided I took James off Vallergan, she would get help for him in the classroom. She said he was so bright, and such a lovely boy, it was a shame for him to be on this drug. What a wonderful person. It worked, he was only just five years old, and without this help so much education would have been lost.

The school at that time was just around the corner from our home. Graham passed us one morning with his latest woman as we were walking towards the school, his head flung back in laughter, as they drove by.

This school was my children's first school and was on the edge of Hitchin. It would be three years before we could make our move to Letchworth.

Chapter Nine

During those three years we had endured a lot. Monthly maintenance cheques often bounced, it was hard to live on my part time wages. I found a good solicitor to start the process of divorce.

In the hallway of the Hitchin courts, Graham had arrived and turned his head not speaking. The court clerk looked sympathetically at me and said, "some people are very difficult". He was trying to be kind and it did help a little.

Once inside and standing before the judge, the rather old looking judge turned to me, "Where is your wedding ring Mrs Daniels?" the judge asked me sternly. "You are not divorced yet," he said.

That day was our first step towards being divorced. The stress within my body was terrible. Afterwards I went to pick the children up from school, I took our dog Max with me to give him a run and to be able to get the children to play on the field a little longer. I needed to breathe, to de-stress, tears were in my eyes and I was swallowing hard.

Lack of money, asthma and eczema, now divorce. Managing my job with the help of a childminder, sometimes sick children, and always wondering if his next cheque would clear was so difficult. My poor mum was sending me occasional letters, written in a spidery scrawl which I could just understand. She used to have the most beautiful handwriting, with wonderful majestic letter "M"s.

I wrote often to her, but only at the very last moment telling her that I was now on my own. I didn't have the money to be able to travel and see her. We did manage some phone calls, which I made to her care home, and that was both lovely and sad.

About a year after Graham left, I went on a rare night out. One of my girlfriends used to make sure I got out of the house every fortnight or so. On this particular occasion we were meeting up with other friends at a party in one of the nearby villages. A tall slim guy with a beard and pleasant smile, came over and chatted me up. He was actually very nice, but he was six years younger than me.

Suffice to say that I did eventually start seeing him, and for around three years he would come and see me a couple of times a week. When I moved to Letchworth, he helped me, and on the weekends that Graham took the children, he and I would travel to see his friends or visit his parents. I suppose I was glad of his company but he had no life experience yet, - he was an only child and although his parents were always lovely to me, they must have wished for him to meet a single girl who hadn't started a family yet.

I don't think either of us was very committed to the relationship, he was not a natural with children for a start. He was clearly still enjoying being single, and I had no problem with that as I wouldn't have wanted to live with another Graham type. I think we were both good for each other for that moment in time.

For a brief period, after our move to Letchworth, I worked for Graham's paternal nan in the family business. It was after I bought the Maxi car from my girlfriend. Nan had weighed up that I now lived close to her factory. Her only son had taken ill and was on medical leave. She asked me to consider going to work for her.

I decided to accept her offer but it was a mistake. Firstly, the "work" was of little value, my rather active brain needed much more than typing the odd letter, or indeed typing several letters which were exactly the same except for the company names and addresses.

Nan also tried to stop me seeing my boyfriend, she used a touch of blackmail. "You can't keep this job if you continue the relationship"

Chapter Nine

Wow! I took the night to consider what nan had said and the next morning I firmly told her that my private life was my own. I would be more than happy to resign!

She obviously hadn't expected this response, she apologised and stressed that she needed me to stay. In all honesty I think she was just using my presence to wind up certain staff. Her son had become ill, he was off work and battling cancer. It was as if she needed a shield in order to stay in charge without her dear son's help.

I managed to do a couple more months of this brain numbing work, before going for an interview which changed my whole life. I should say at this point that there were at least two members of staff who would definitely look after nan. They were very loyal and I knew that she would in fact be perfectly fine without me there.

Chapter Ten

I arrived promptly at a factory on the edge of the industrial estate in Baldock.

A large Scottish man introduced himself to me and showed me to an office. At that time the single storey building had several rooms with a passageway to the left of them. There were only one or two old machines which were worked by hand, a couple of mills and a lathe.

After a fairly straightforward interview, I was introduced to a tall thin man with black, short, hair and a mustache. He was wearing a work coat and was drawing on a roll up which was threatening to set his mustache alight. We shook hands, then a much more smartly dressed man entered the office.

I noted his highly polished brown boots, a rather plush patterned jumper, and metal rimmed glasses to his face. We too shook hands. These guys were all happy, smiling, individuals. You could somehow tell they were interesting and "no nonsense" sort of people. I liked them, I also liked the work on offer. I have always had a love of bookkeeping.

It would be a few days before I would hear whether or not I got the job. I was back up north for a wedding, when the call came through.

I had given my brother's phone number to the company, and I was so happy to get good news, but now I had to hand my notice in to nan. Luckily my children kept me busy on the train journey back home, (my car would not have made it that far), so I couldn't overthink how I was going to handle nan.

It was difficult to explain about my new employment, without hurting her feelings. Nan could be petulant! However, by the end of the week she seemed better, - I had played heavily on my need to get more experience in bookkeeping, to help my chances of improving my wage in the years ahead.

My first morning driving to my new job I was so excited that I even made the children excited for me. I dropped them at their different schools early and headed into Baldock.

Two of the three men that I'd met at my interview greeted me, apparently the other was still working out his notice at a position in Africa. The job was easy for me, the company had only just started up. They opened in May of 1985 and I had started my part time job in late June, and so the phones were not that busy and the paperwork was sparse. Both men worked hard and were jovial and very amusing at break times. The tall, slim, chap had left his family behind in order to get the firm up and running. I can't now remember where his family lived, but they were a hundred or so miles away. He was therefore living at the home of his friend, who was still in Africa, whom I met at my interview.

During the first two months that the company traded the Scottish man's wife had dealt with the books. Because I was not busy initially,

Chapter Ten

I decided to look over her work and her filing system to make sure that I could fit in easily with the system.

I did have to make some small adjustments, but more worrying to me, I discovered odd transactions.

A carpet for the small office had been purchased. I can't remember the value now, but it was a lot and that fact made me look at the invoice. The carpet was dimensionally very large and had been delivered to a director's home. The office was benefiting from an offcut of that carpet.

A lawnmower had been bought, but there was no grass here to cut. Worse still, petrol was not only filling up both of the couples cars, but was filling up several cans too, all listed separately on the invoice. Their cars were both on lease to them, being paid for by the company, starting at the end of May. This information would not have mattered if all three men had invested into the company equally, and were equally drawing wages, but this was not so.

The guy in Africa, called Laurie, had invested thirty thousand pounds. The Scottish couple invested a few hundred pounds, and were drawing a wage each with extra perks. Trevor had invested the least, but was not taking a wage.

I spent a day or two wondering how to manage my knowledge. Was it any of my business?

I decided to do a three month report and provide each director with a copy. If they weren't bothered by the high fuel cost, or the purchase of a lawnmower and very expensive carpet, then fine.

I gave two reports to my boss so that he could give Trevor his. I decided to give Laurie his when he finally started working with us. That would be in two week's time.

My boss did actually flush red, he said he would look at them first, before handing Trevor his.

During the next two weeks I had to go into hospital for a planned operation. I was now thirty four and was about to have an operation on my deaf ear. Twenty three years after losing most of my hearing in that ear.

There were three of us on the ward having the same operation. A cut behind the ear to gain entry to the canal. They would take a small piece of skin from the surface area, to be used to replace my eardrum.

Whilst they were doing this, they discovered that I was missing three of the vital bones which formed the hearing system. They were able to replace two of these with a plastic version.

When I came to, I was advised not to move and to keep my face on the pillow. Any need for the toilet meant using the bedpan for two days. Two days!! I thought I would be going straight home. My children were with their aunty Glenda, we both thought I would be home. I had to get back to my new job. Luckily Glenda is a competent person. She shared the childminding with my sister over the next few days. She phoned my office. My boss and Trevor actually visited me in the hospital.

When the surgeon told me of my missing bones within the ear, my mind went back to when I visited a Hitchin doctor in 1971. She had syringed that ear saying I must have wax build up. Perhaps she washed the bones away.

Then there was the time I almost drowned. Graham and I had gone to the Blue Lagoon near Arlesey. He could swim like a fish and I couldn't swim at all. So I never ever put my head below the water surface. However, the lagoon was actually a gravel pit. After the first two meters entry into the water the ground dropped away completely.

As Graham swam towards a friend I walked forward in the water to follow. Suddenly I was flailing my arms and legs. I could only see greyness all around, as I held my breath, panic rose immediately.

Chapter Ten

I felt what I knew to be a body in front of me, I clawed at it trying to pull myself upwards. Two hands gripped my arms and pulled me to the surface, it was Graham. I had scratched the middle of his chest as he swam down to find me.

So maybe this incident was when I lost the bones in my ear.

After the yachting and the "drowning" moment I went on to learn how to swim. I'm not a strong swimmer, but once I could swim, I went back to the gravel pit and swam slowly out to the crane in the middle of the lagoon, - I sat on it and rested, before swimming back again to the grass covered edge. Graham and someone else, I can't now remember who, had swum either side of me, just in case.

The other women on my ward were doing well like myself, but sadly one of them lost the feeling within her cheek. Her face was dropped on one side. "That could have been me", I remember thinking.

I was glad to get home and to have my children back. Once I was home, I apologised profusely for being away much longer than expected. A day or two had turned into a week. My sister and sister-in-law were very good about it. My bosses were very kind.

Over the next few weeks I was happy to find that my hearing had improved by around sixty per cent.

There was no discussion about my three month financial report, and I had no idea whether Trevor had been given his copy.

The business was trading fairly well, both men had worked together at a Luton company beforehand, and they knew what they were doing. It was also where they met Laurie, and had become good friends and drinking partners. Over time they made a plan to get their own business and apparently as Laurie fell out of love with Africa, he pushed their idea forward. He found a factory to rent, some old machines to buy, and then they simply gave notice to their employer. My main boss Mark was clearly a driving force and was the only one going out and getting orders for the company. But his financial input was next to nothing and he and his wife were happily drawing on Laurie's investment, for more than just wages, whereas Trevor was drawing nothing to start with.

After I made the coffee one morning, I went to the one toilet in the building that we all shared.

Oh heck! The largest turd in the world was sitting there.

Should I go and tell them, get them to sort it out? Shall I just flush it away. Well of course, no fuss just flush it away. Oh no!! It didn't move.

I tried another flush. It was still there. What to do?. I'd have to tell them, a customer might need to use the toilet. I still hadn't relieved myself, but feeling embarrassed I went into the office to tell Mark.

He immediately sped off to the loo to deal with it. A few short minutes later he came back gushing about his success. "its gone, I cut it up wi' a wee saw blade" he told me in his best broad Scottish accent. Oh gosh, how I laughed. And now, I still had to go to the toilet.

He was very amusing. He told me once that his dead mother came to his bedroom and stood at the bottom of his bed. That was why he had a completely white lock of hair to the front of his head. I'm not sure I believed him.

Laurie completed his contract in Africa and started working with us sometime in August. After a couple of days I handed him his financial folder with the first three months breakdown. Bedtime reading he called it. His girlfriend came in to see him at lunch time. She was a pretty girl, slim, dark hair, and had a rather pale complexion.

Chapter Ten

I felt she was unhappy. She certainly didn't talk much. I later understood that she was ready to move on from their relationship. He had done years of six weeks working abroad, then six weeks at home, and it was getting her down.

The next day was shocking for me. Mark was not in when I arrived, only Trevor. Trevor said that Mark had not given him his copy of the accounts. He said that when Laurie read his copy he was furious. Trevor had to read Laurie's copy to understand his fury. As Trevor was living with Laurie this all happened in minutes. Trevor too was completely shocked. As an equal partner, he had no idea of how Mark was draining the funds. They went to Mark's house to have a meeting.

It did not end well for Mark, he was told to stay away and their friendship was shattered forever.

Trevor explained that Laurie was now at the garage where the couples cars were being leased from. His aim was to put a stop on our company account to prevent further purchases, and to cancel the lease contracts made using our company name. They could of course keep the cars in their own names.

I took all of this information in, and although I knew that what Mark and his wife had done was a bit dodgy, I felt terrible.

Laurie did come into work after dealing with the various matters. He'd had to go to the bank too. Oh dear!

Laurie now had to step up to the plate to find work. He did well, and he and Trevor were busy most of the time. I forgot that Laurie had personal problems too, he did not chat in the way that Mark did, and after all that had happened, I was relieved to be busy outside of work. I was still seeing my boyfriend, so life was moving along quite well for the children and me.

63

Graham was having the children to stay, once a month, for a weekend, which gave me some free time.

About two weeks after Mark was dealt with, Laurie took a day off, and Trevor told me that sadly Laurie's relationship was over. His partner was moving back to Norfolk.

The atmosphere took another dip for a week or two. I didn't know Laurie well enough to be able to say anything of comfort to him, Trevor did his best to stay cheerful and I know he too was glad to go home at the weekends to see his wife and family.

Two more weeks on and we had all settled down from the various problems. Trevor was full of good humour, he was very proud of his family. I think they were at college at this point in time. I believe his son became a very accomplished clothes designer.

One morning after our first coffee break, Laurie came up to me holding a small piece of metal in his fingers, and playing nervously with it. "Would you like to go out for dinner with me tonight?"

Well, I was so shocked. I looked away, and started pulling desk drawers open as if looking for something. I seem to remember muttering that I had a boyfriend, that it was nice of him to ask me. I was very flustered. I don't remember what else was said, but I really was not expecting this at all. Laurie asked me to think about it.

Over the next few days, I found it impossible to forget about the possibility of a date with Laurie. I weighed up that if I finished my three year relationship, and went out with Laurie, I might find myself on my own again, if we didn't hit it off.

I reasoned that I already knew my present relationship wasn't going anywhere, neither of us were that committed to each other. He lived twenty miles away, and in three years we had not moved the relationship forwards. I took courage and phoned my boyfriend.

Chapter Ten

I explained how I felt and said that we should part ways.

When I was able to tell Laurie that I was free to go on a dinner date if he still wanted to, he said he would pick me up that Saturday.

I organised a childminder, and that Saturday we enjoyed dinner out together. He was full of chatter about Africa.

With Graham, I had been on a rollercoaster, unable to believe him, unsure where we would move to next, emotionally drained as I tried to be a mother and a father. Making decisions on my own regarding their poor health, the schools, how to protect them from cruel comments. James endured so much because of the rough skin on his hands .

Now we would have a period of calm, family and home wise. Laurie loved his home, he had purchased a detached house only eighteen months before I met him. There would be no moving around for him. He was a hard working, determined, quiet man. His quirky sense of humor and love of traveling appealed to me.

So when our relationship developed and we spent more time together at each other's homes, and the children seemed fairly ok with Laurie being around, I happily continued becoming drawn into a deeper, secure, situation.

Three months on from our first date, it was Christmas and it was my turn to do the dinner for all of the family. Despite the separation, divorce, and then Graham remarrying, his family had continued to have the children and I to dinner on Christmas day. We had always taken it in turn, and it was great fun. Each new born child added to the numbers as each year passed. I'm pretty sure I did dinner for fourteen on the last occasion, because we had Laurie and Graham plus his new wife.

My home was not huge and my table only sat six or seven people around it. Laurie completely surprised me by wanting to spend Christmas with us, I really thought he would be with his sister or brother and parents. He said he would transport his large conservatory table to mine plus chairs. Looking back I have no idea how we fitted it all in, but I recall that we managed and it went quite well. This year Graham and his wife were on their own, as her children were with their father, and so they were joining us.

I hardly noticed the barbed comments from Graham's wife, because Laurie was so helpful and kind, helping the conversation to flow well. Laurie loved socialising, and had many great stories, amazingly he was good with the children too.

At his house, the week before, we were spending the weekend with him. Suddenly, an open lorry pulled into his drive, swung around the almond shaped island of grass, pointing back out towards the road again. A guy stepped out of the cab, jumped up onto a pile of huge Christmas trees, picked one up and flung it onto the drive by the front door. He then jumped down, got back into his cab and drove off. My children were beside themselves with excitement. Laurie had organised this for them. It was fourteen feet high. We all pulled it into the large hallway, Laurie stood it up against the corner of the stairs so that it spanned the ground floor and stretched up into the first floor.

We had so much fun decorating it and it was such a lovely thing for Laurie to have done. My kids would never forget, it was a forever memory.

At my house, when the family left after helping to clear up the Christmas mess, Laurie stayed on and we enjoyed a lovely late afternoon with the children. Then he had to get back to his pets as they had been left on their own for some four or five hours.

Chapter Ten

Over the next few months, orders came in quite well, and we were kept busy. I was introduced to Laurie's parents, his friends, his siblings and a nephew and niece, the oldest, Lisa, being thirteen years old.

We went out with my friends and eventually travelled north to visit my brothers, and my mum who was in a home.

We enjoyed many lovely holidays in the UK, the Lake District, Devon, Derbyshire, -taking all three dogs with us, traveling in two cars. Laurie had two dogs and I had Max. Trevor looked after Laurie's home, the business and his African grey parrots.

We went to Malta where I took the children trekking on horseback, sadly Laurie didn't ride nor did he want to try.

My first attempt at horse riding was when I was about ten or eleven I think. As children in those days, we were encouraged to "go out and play". I walked across several fields caught up in my own thoughts. In one of these fields was an older horse called Peggy. One day I simply decided to jump on her back, and holding on to her mane we moved off jumping over the occasional nettle patch which blocked our way. This was very naughty, though I didn't consider that at the time. Later my dad took me to meet the farmer who owned the horse, the farmer saddled her up, showed me how to hold the reins and led me back to her field.

I rode around and jumped some very low proper fencing. Another young lady of around seventeen years old, then took over from me. She could really ride. In fact she rode Peggy at the Durham horse show that year. Fancy that, my first ride had been on a proper show jumper, and because I shouldn't have done it I couldn't tell anyone.

I rode Peggy occasionally over the next year or two but I wouldn't call myself a competent rider.

I recall the farmer asking me to follow his herd of cattle one day with Peggy. He was leading the herd on foot from the milking sheds, onto the main village road, about half a mile through the village to a nice lush field of grass.

I was to follow behind and keep them moving. Everything went perfectly and I was enjoying this outing,- I was about thirteen years old and as the traffic slowly built up behind us, I felt slightly embarrassed. I could see that the farmer was directing the cattle into a field about a hundred yards ahead of me. (This is my guess today from that memory).

There was a red bus in the traffic full of early morning passengers. Suddenly, two cows started rushing to their left and dashed through an open gate into a field. Oh no!

Quickly I urged Peggy forward so as to prevent any further runaways. Then, once they passed the gate, I made the split decision to enter the field and try to round up the two cows. This could have been a disaster. A whole field to mess me about. However, as I rode in a circle around them, they trotted speedily back to the gate and joined the herd, making it look like I was very professional, and was an expert child cowgirl.

As Peggy and I trotted past the bus the passengers stood up and clapped us, I went bright red and was so relieved to join the farmer who by now had all of the cows into his field. Phew!

Chapter Eleven

On our visit to Malta we met and made a long time friendship with Joe, a Maltese man of around thirty five years old who worked on the beach and in the hotel at night.

Whilst there Joe took us to his home where we met his mum and sisters.

Although we exchanged contact details, we didn't know if we would ever meet again.

Two years after that lovely holiday, there was a knock on my office door. We had purchased a second building by now, adjoining our first factory. I was now in an upstairs office, above a large reception area. It was Joe. And behind him was Laurie, beaming happily.

"He just parked a huge lorry by the side of Tesco" he said. " He's delivering sugar to Tesco, from Bury St Edmunds."

Good grief. This was his winter job. He had told us about it when we were on holiday. He passed over a carrier bag containing a couple of broken bags of sugar. We had coffee, and reminisced but Joe had to get back to the lorry. We insisted that he should come to the house and go out with us that evening. Besides, the children had such a great holiday in Malta, mainly because of Joe who manned the water sports, that he had to see the kids at least. He agreed, the children loved seeing him again. It was bonfire night, and we were going to some friends to watch the local fireworks from their bedroom window. Their house backed onto the football field where the fire would be lit and a wonderful display of fireworks provided. Joe loved it, - we had shared viewing fireworks in his village when in Malta. Those fireworks had huge bangs and one bright light. Ours were a bit quieter, but lasted so much longer and of course were more colourful.

We saw a lot of Joe over the years. He married an English woman at Bury St Edmunds, and we went to their wedding. After they moved back to Malta, we managed another visit to them, taking my step ex mother-in-law with us. We had been on holiday together that year. My marriage had been over for twenty years by now, but I still saw and got on well with all of his family.

Laurie loved Spain and we bought a timeshare there. I think we owned it for about twenty odd years. He liked the assurance of knowing it would be clean and well kept year after year. The restaurant was excellent and the entertainment was of good quality.

Singers, comedians, and flamenco dancers were provided a couple of nights a week and because it was a small resort we felt pretty comfortable there.

And so our lives merged, his friends, my friends, sharing holidays and family events such as birthdays and christenings, though we took twelve years before we decided to get married.

I loved listening to Laurie's stories of adventure, his father had insisted that he do an apprenticeship, and he chose engineering. Later when his first marriage failed, he was free to choose to engage in dangerous, well paid work. He started off working on the oil rigs in the North Sea. In those days he told me that in order to get to the rig from the boat which they travelled on, they had to throw their bags into a rope cage which was placed on deck from a hovering helicopter. Then they had to cling to the side of the cage and brace, as the helicopter took up the slack when the boat he was on dipped down with the waves.

Then he was whisked upwards, hanging on tightly, before being lowered onto the rig platform. He would let go and then grab his bag before signaling that he was ok.

He loved the camaraderie, the characters he met, and the socialising after a hard day. He drank and smoked quite heavily in those days.

During our first two years together, he often took himself off to see one of these friends and his wife. The guy was still working on the rigs and on his time off Laurie found time to have a drinking session with him somewhere in Norfolk.

One terrible day, we had a call from his friend's wife to say there had been a dreadful incident. A sudden blowout had burst into flames, catching her husband in amongst it. They had to quickly helicopter him to the burns unit. He lasted a day or two, his lips had melted and sadly his lungs were badly damaged. Of course Laurie left straight away to do what he could, it was devastating for the family. When Laurie came home he was so sad, and of course he had to return there for the funeral.

It had been some years since Laurie had worked on those rigs. During his last few years of working for other companies, he had been working for an oil company, on the West Coast of Africa, assisting with setting up new oil production within the country.

Initially he was on his own within a fenced camp. Monitoring and keeping everything safe until production would start. After six weeks another guy would arrive to take over, and Laurie would be home for six weeks.

This was the schedule that ruined his ten year relationship with his girlfriend and something that I never had to endure. But the stories he told me are in my heart forever.

He fed the local animals that visited the camp. He would wake up, throw the door of his small building open and find a deer and birds waiting for him and the food which he would give them. He rescued a tiny, bald, baby monkey from the villagers outside of his camp. The locals had killed its mother to eat so Laurie had bartered for its life with bananas.

He said this tiny thing fitted into the palm of his hand, he fed it with baby formula milk using a small pipette.

This tiny monkey thrived and thought of Laurie as his mum. Eventually covered in hair and growing well, Laurie named him Mr John, and entrusted his work colleague to care for him on his six week return to England. This worked well for a long time.

When at work, during his break times, Laurie would drive off into the forest in his land rover, Mr John would sit on his shoulder. Then when they stopped, Mr John would run off into the trees with Laurie watching him. When he came back and sat on Laurie's arm, he was mischievously thrown into the river by Laurie. Furious with his "mum" Mr John would sulk and turn his back to ignore Laurie. A few thrown pebbles to tease him and change his mood did not work either. But when Laurie turned on the engine of the land rover and eased back along the track, Mr John could be seen by Laurie in his wing mirror, scooting frantically alongside, before he leapt up and took his position on Laurie's shoulder once more.

Chapter Eleven

Around the time of my interview, when I briefly met Laurie, he was considering trying to bring Mr John home to England. A couple of years previously he had brought back two baby African Grey parrots which he called Big 'un and Little 'un. When I first moved in with Laurie he had two dogs and these two parrots. I had one dog, one cat, gerbils, and two children, as he would often tell people.

The last time Laurie got back to the camp in Africa all was not well. One of the villagers had entered the camp, stolen Mr John and I'm afraid, eaten him. I really can't imagine how Laurie must have felt. He was very bitter and must have been glad that his time in Africa was ending. Oh dear!

During our first year together Laurie wanted the children and I to move in with him. He persuaded me to purchase my home and then rent it out.

I was nervous about this because I just knew that the tenants might be great, but they might also be a pain. The first lot were the latter but thankfully they didn't stay too long. My second attempt with tenants was better. A single lady with children, and she was very tidy and punctual with her rent.

This first year I met most of Laurie's family, a sister and rather ebullient husband with two children who lived in Letchworth and who therefore saw quite a lot of Laurie. I also met his brother and sister-in-law, who lived quite near his parents and who had no children of their own at this point. We didn't see his brother much, but we travelled often at weekends to see his parents who lived in Greenford, London.

My sister lived within a mile of Laurie's house after her marriage, and so I often had her and her husband and daughter over for Sunday dinner.

During our second year together we took a holiday in the Lake District and on the way home when the holiday was over, Laurie suggested that we do a slight detour and see my mum in her care home. This was so thoughtful of him, I hadn't thought it possible because of the distance and because he did all of the driving on this holiday. It was a lovely visit, my mum was in the grip of dementia but she loved seeing the children, she was cheerful and chatted to Laurie. I had already been writing about my situation in my letters to her and it was good to know that she understood. I noted how her head was now permanently inclined to one side. My heart broke for her.

Laurie teased me on the way home that he now knew where I got my chubby cheeks from. I was emotional and cried quietly, trying not to let the children see. I was thrilled that Laurie had enabled us to see mum, but I could also see how much she had deteriorated.

Three months later she died.

Mum died between Christmas and the new year. That year we'd had Laurie's parents to stay with us for Christmas. I had been laid up in bed with the flu when the call from my brother's wife came. I had managed to cook and join in on Christmas day but by boxing day I was ill. It was a miserable few days as no one wanted to catch my germs, even the children stood in the doorway to see me. Then came the phone call with the news that mum had passed away.

By New Year's Eve the flu symptoms were much better and Laurie persuaded me to go to the pub with him and Trevor, leaving the children with his parents.

Chapter Eleven

It was miserable, I was glad to leave the house but just couldn't get into the high spirits of it.
So the year started with mum's funeral.

It was a terrible year globally too. The world was in the grip of a very bad recession. Trevor made the decision to leave and resigned from the company to find more solid work. At some point in the next year or two, Laurie also went to work elsewhere leaving me to run the business. Then at another point, having made and saved more money, he was back at the helm, and I worked elsewhere for five or six months to save drawing wages and to earn independently. I caught up with the company bookwork during weekends. The struggle to stay in business during these years was incredibly difficult.

Chapter Twelve

Years previously, after Graham and Alan lost their mum, their father continued living at the family home.

Eventually though, everything had to change. Alan and Janet married and after spending time at the family home, they now moved into rented accommodation. Their father married again. His new wife was the daughter of the late proprietor of the Fishing Gazette. The paper was originally founded by her grandfather, who edited the paper for many years. Then his two sons continued on with the paper. When Pats' father died, she kept the paper going for a while and through her work and family, she would often meet Graham's father at various fishing events. So they knew each other quite well, and he also wrote fishing articles for her paper.

These were happy years for the family. Graham's dad and his new, younger wife Pat, decided to have a child. Alan and Janet already had Iaan and followed with a second child a few years later. Glenda and her husband had a little girl. Graham and I had moved to Ipswich but had returned with our own little girl, and after another three years we had James.

At Letchworth, nan was now a great-grandmother five times over.

I have mentioned nan's rather spoilt nature regarding when she wrote a cookery book, just to prove she was as able as Elsa. Well she had also complained considerably at not having many photographs taken of her at Graham and my wedding. I hardly knew what to say as I had let the photographer do his job. Nan was the last person on my mind that day.

Now her son had found another lady to share his life with and at first nan appeared happy, but jealousy soon set in. Luckily as she and her son worked together, any problems between the women were smoothed over daily by him. There followed many years of business events that the three of them went to. It wasn't all about fishing. The family business manufactured lawn mowers and sold them to golf clubs, councils, and race courses as well as the general public.

There were many happy family Christmas meals, where Pat would cook and take food over to nan's house for the whole family to enjoy. I think she worked hard to fit in and having their own child was a blessing for them. Graham and I liked her and we were pleased to hear of her pregnancy.

Over the many years, barring a few hiccups, Pat has been helpful, advisory, and has joined in on almost all family events.

When her husband died, I had just started seeing Laurie, who sadly did not get to meet him as the illness had progressed to a terminal stage. Laurie was a fan of his fishing abilities and having fished as a young man himself, he was well aware of him. He had made quite a name for himself.

Chapter Twelve

We always included Pat in our family events, she was my children's step grandmother, and her son, only nine at the time of his father's death, was my children's uncle.

Having endured the loss of her only son, nan's companion Elsa also died. We all attended her funeral in Luton. It was held there because Elsa had made friends at the Luton church and had attended it regularly over many years.

We went through a period of engaging more help for nan, spending nights with nan when we had no one to help. Each of us shared scary stories of our nights in her tudor home. It was haunted. Mostly it was just creaky floor boards or noisy old heating pipes. But one morning when I was there, nan asked me to get her suit which was hanging up on the wardrobe door in the haunted bedroom. I don't believe in ghosts and thought nothing of crossing the landing into the room. Suddenly, I hit a wall of ice. I couldn't move. I could see the suit, I could feel the cold. Mustering all my resolve, I pushed forward, stretched out my hand and grabbed the suit before turning and running from the room.

We finally found a live-in housekeeper to help nan who seemed quite good. However, nan decided, after a few months, to move members of the family in with herself. She chose Graham and his wife. They were the only ones who could leave their accommodation and move in easily. The family could see the sense of it as it took the pressure and worry off our shoulders, but Graham? Seriously!!

Nan had stopped going into work by now, she missed her son so much and was frail from sadness.

After only a few months of going to live with nan, the new housekeeper soon resigned her position. One of nan's cleaning ladies befriended Graham and his wife. Needless to say I didn't feel comfortable visiting nan anymore, but I was to find out later that none of the family felt welcome and that they also felt uncomfortable when they visited.

It was really nothing to do with me, I had helped as much as I could, so I got on with looking after Laurie, our home, and my children.

One day after I had dropped the children at school, Laurie phoned to say that Cass, one of his dogs, had run off. He spent over an hour driving around our village, scouring the fields, but there was no sign of the dog. Just after lunch, Hitchin police station rang to say they had picked up our dog. They had fed him and there would be a fee to pay when we picked him up. Because Laurie had already lost time from work that morning, I offered to go and get Cass.

Feeling happy to have Cass in my car I headed for home and decided it wasn't worth going back to work. I would do some housework before picking up the children. I indicated left, slowed right down and swung the car into our drive. I had to brake suddenly because there in front of me was Graham's wife and nan's housekeeper. I wound my window down and said "what the hell are you doing in our drive". The housekeeper looked sheepish and fled back out of the entrance. Graham's wife just laughed and slowly joined the other lady.

I quickly parked, grabbed Cass and went inside of the house. My God, the nerve. I looked out of the living room window and saw that both had returned and the wife was taking pictures of our home.

They left pretty quickly after taking a few shots, and I phoned my solicitor to have a note made of the incident. There was an ongoing maintenance case and we were due at court soon. Graham's cheques rarely arrived and in any case they hardly ever cleared to put funds in my account.

Chapter Twelve

One morning, I got a call from the family, nan had passed during the night. I felt sad especially as quality time spent with her had been taken away by Graham's decision to move in with her. He hardly ever kept a job and moving in with nan using her food and energy would have suited him very well.

Some time after her funeral, the family called a meeting which included me.

"He promised me he would behave," Alan said. "I will never speak to him again "

"What's happened?" I asked.

From each and everyone of the family, including the brother's step-mum Pat, poured stories of how nan stopped wanting to see them. How the housekeepers had left, how they thought Graham had taken over the household accounts.

Graham told them that he was the only beneficiary in nan's will.

Worse still, over the years nan had become dependent on Mogadon. The family doctor, an old trusting chap, gave her a new prescription a few days before she died.

The older brother Richard said, "Something is very wrong, nan advised me some time ago that after losing dad, she was going to leave something to all of his children"

I remembered nan saying this myself, it wasn't just about money, she wanted her company shares to be divided amongst the family too.

Richard was so angry and had spent some days mulling over options. This was going to be very expensive, involving solicitors.

None of us were particularly flush with money at this point in our lives.

His plan was to use either his daughter or mine and try to get legal aid through them.

I had to say that I couldn't let this happen to my daughter. "This is her dad, I can't let this come between them" I said. They all understood and they decided to at least take action to hold Graham up from executing the will. A solicitors letter was sent.

A few weeks later after a tragedy had befallen one of Richard's friends, he phoned me to say that his heart was no longer in it, to contest the will.

I of course had been speaking with Laurie over the weeks. He suggested that I at least talk to my solicitor to explain what was going on, especially as he was fighting in court for my maintenance for the children. The solicitor thought a few enquiring letters to Graham's solicitor might be an idea. We had already held up Graham from getting probate so there was every reason to push a little harder.

Within two weeks letters were going backwards and forwards and then, eureka! A breakthrough!.

Graham's side included not only a copy of the will, but a copy of the solicitors notes, written up late at night after drawing up a changed will, only two or three days before nan died. The will and notes had arrived attached to a letter answering one of my solicitor's questions.

Nan was suffering from a severe cold and Graham urged the solicitor to get the will typed up the same day. He did as he was asked and returned the next day for nan to sign the will. I think he took two staff members to witness the signing. Clearly he was troubled by all of this and meticulously made notes to cover himself.

Nan died only a day later.

When her doctor was called and he had pronounced nan dead, he collected her remaining mogadon tablets. Some were unaccounted for, but had apparently been taken by family members to help them sleep.

Chapter Twelve

Papers were prepared, and all supporting evidence was sent to a barrister in London for advice. I was made aware of the costs so far. If we had no case we could at least pay so far.

Both sets of solicitors were now all waiting on our barrister. Graham, his brothers and their wives plus myself were all on tenterhooks for different reasons.

The barrister's advice eventually arrived. Meticulous and well pondered. He concluded that we had a reasonable case and because of those included notes from the other side's solicitor, a chance at least of a good outcome for our side. He had to caution us that if I were to be the one to contest the will, it could be argued that I was a bitter wife causing trouble and being vengeful.

Laurie and I had a lot to talk about.

He wanted me to pursue the matter, I was concerned about the costs. How would I pay if we lost the case? The bill could be in the hundreds of thousands if we went ahead.

After a few sleepless nights I resolved to fight. I had a wonderful solicitor, the barrister seemed pretty good to me, and I decided to put my own house on the line as collateral for my solicitors. Laurie was behind me one hundred per cent, which helped enormously. Even more helpful, I was not asked to pay as we went along, the bill grew month after month and would be settled at the end. Oh my Lord!!

Chapter Thirteen

There followed a long period of preparation for the court case. It would be heard at the Royal Courts of Justice in London.

We had to phone or write to everyone who knew nan. My solicitor had to write to her doctor, the undertaker, past housekeepers. The task was huge.

A year into all of this preparation we were advised by someone that Graham had to take a job. He couldn't get his hands on nan's money or assets any more. They had to survive until the court case settled. This advice led my solicitor to find out who was now employing him. I decided to make a call to this company, suggested by a solicitor, along the lines of gathering information for an important court case.

Wow. They talked. The main guy seemed very nice, he was happy to spill that Graham was a boastful man. They were all fully aware of the impending court case. Graham told the guy how he frightened away the housekeepers. He gloated about the change of nan's will and that he had already sold thousands of pounds worth of items.

I relayed this conversation to my solicitor. He wanted the guy to volunteer to make a statement, and of course come to court. I made another telephone call, but this gentleman now showed his hand. He wanted a large sum of money to help me. I turned him down and advised my solicitor.

A few weeks later I was astonished to hear that Graham had to go to the police. The guy at work, having failed to extort money from me, was now blackmailing him.

The police and he set up a plan to reveal the blackmail. Graham was wired up by the police. He was to meet his boss at a supermarket car park, with a requested amount of money. I don't know if he actually had money with him, I suggest he didn't. But enough was spoken about in the car, for the police to make an arrest. I can't tell you how astonished I was about this, and how glad I was that I had backed away from this guy some weeks earlier.

Eventually all that could be done to present our case, was completed.
It must have taken a couple of years, I can't remember now. Laurie and I travelled on the train from Hitchin to London with my solicitor. The solicitor was calm and in good humour, but I was nervous. I really didn't enjoy seeing Graham anymore. The tall buildings and noise of London wrapped around me. Once inside the Royal Courts of Justice, it became quieter and businesslike.

I thought to myself how light it was inside of the building. I hardly remember how we got to our seats, my solicitor making sure that Laurie and I were seated and ready. He began conversing with our barrister.

Chapter Thirteen

My solicitor turned to me and said, "Graham's wife has brought her own solicitor". Things were about to start, I would have to understand this piece of news later.

Each side presented their case. Witnesses were called and made their statements, some were questioned. The judge had read those important notes regarding how the final will came to be. Two of Graham's witnesses were found to be unreliable under oath, and his case floundered. The judge ordered the family to come together and to fairly agree on an outcome regarding the estate. Graham's solicitor would leave him in no doubt that he had lost, as ours also told us that we had won, but we must try to come to an arrangement. An irritated judge might make a ruling that would leave everyone upset.

The whole family walked behind and alongside our solicitor. He led us from the court building to much quieter and almost deserted streets where all of the barristers had their offices. I remembered thinking how beautiful the buildings were. A few men and women passed us wearing their wigs and gowns, obviously heading for the court.

We reached a waiting room, with offices leading off from it. Laurie and I listened carefully to the barrister and our solicitor. We were directed to allocate a sum to Graham, then the bills would be paid, and finally each member of the family would equally split the rest.

It might seem unfair that Graham should still profit, especially in the light of alleged wrongdoings, but that is how it works. Find a solution, or the judge will rule. He might go back several years to a previous will, where maybe nothing was left to any family member.

I went into the waiting room to call in the family, the barrister left and all questions were directed at our solicitor.

Finally, a figure was put before Graham's solicitor who was presumably in another building nearby. Eventually there was agreement.

The solicitors costs on both sides were taken into account and we all felt that the remaining amount to be split between the family was acceptable. There was a matter of the company shares to be allocated, which we did fairly quickly, refusing to give any to Graham.

We think that Graham's wife took her own solicitor in order to negotiate with him separately regarding the money passed his way.

When we returned to the court, his wife had to go past me in a small aisle. She took the opportunity to swing her fist against my hand as it rested by my thigh. I was furious and turned to my solicitor, but he said to stay calm and ignore it.

All formalities took place and the judge commended the family for coming to a resolution. It was over.

There was a period of peace for myself now. I had done months, if not years, of working for Laurie and then plowing through paperwork for the court case in the evenings. I had long conversations with Nan's friends and work associates. Pat, who knew Nan's relatives and friends much better than I did, put in a lot of work too and took friendly guidance from a retired judge whom she knew. My maintenance fight was on hold until this main case was sorted.

Nan's home would now be vacated by Graham and his family. It had to have the garden overhauled, and I fought for some funds from the solicitor to decorate certain rooms in the house. We only had to paint some walls white.

The house went up for sale. In Letchworth most properties are leasehold, and so we bought the leasehold in order to make it more saleable. It was a grade two listed building, so in order for it to sell in a reasonable time, we did everything possible to make a sale easier.

Chapter Thirteen

When the estate agents were not free for the occasional viewing, I took people around myself.

On one occasion, an Asian lady started to walk up the stairs to the minstrel gallery, when there was a knock at the front door. I went to answer the door, swung it open but there was no one there. I was only three yards from the front door when we heard the knock. From the door to the gated entrance was at least fifteen yards. I stepped out and looked across both sides of the house, there was no-one.

As I closed the door and went towards the stairs to join the lady, she said "Is this house haunted?"

I had to admit that there were claims of it being haunted. She didn't seem worried about it, but it shows the house definitely had that feel to it.

Finally the house sold and life could resume in a more normal way.

A few weeks later my solicitor and I walked into Bedford County Court together.

At last, now that Graham had been allocated money from nan's estate, he could finally pay years of unsettled child maintenance. The judge did not seem too impressed with Graham. I suppose they form an opinion when reading the case notes. Graham arrived on his own without a solicitor.

After listening to the excuses, the judge told him to pay me an amount forthwith or spend time at Her Majesty's pleasure to think about it. Graham said "I'm sorry, what do you mean?"

"I mean you will be taken to prison right now to spend some time assessing your position.

"Oh" said Graham. I have to say, most of the people in the room smiled, including Graham.

A week later after years of no help from my children's father, the rather large cheque arrived. I remember thinking that although it had taken years to sort Graham and his wife out, regarding the will and the children's maintenance, in my case justice was indeed served.

Chapter Fourteen

One of the most positive aspects of living with Laurie was that he really lived life to the full. He was 41 when we first met. I soon discovered that he loved a beer and a laugh with the guys down the pub. If you asked his two African grey parrots "where's Laurie?", they would respond "down the pub". I presume Laurie's partner taught them this, in her many hours of waiting around for him.

Laurie had already worked on the rigs in the North Sea, manned oil stations in Africa, built his own house in London, and recovered from a failed marriage before I had even met him. He had a huge scar down one arm from when he had overdone the drinking, and pushed his arm through a glass door which he didn't realise was there. His brother-in-law said that Laurie could, and did, fall asleep anywhere after a few drinks. There was truth to this, but during the first two years of knowing him, after visiting a consultant on doctors advice, we found out that he was suffering from a condition known as ankylosing spondylitis. This was a very painful condition and had a side effect of tiredness.

Yet every morning Laurie was up early, embracing the day, placing a lovely cup of tea on my bedside table. In the winter months he went shooting with his brother and friends, getting up at a ghastly hour and leaving the house before 7am.

Sometimes I drank the lovely hot tea and went back to sleep and sometimes it was cold long before I saw it.

During the early years of starting his own business, he would often work very late hours to meet customers deadlines. I often cooked his dinner around ten o'clock at night, then covered it and placed it in a warm oven ready for whenever he came in.

Life was always busy, we would visit his mum and dad in London at the weekends, and because he knew so many couples from the pub, there was always a party to go to. He made time for my friends too and indulged in late night drinking with my younger brother on his many visits, down from Durham, to see me.

Laurie and his sister and brother- in-law had purchased static caravans at Frejus near Saint-Tropez. Every summer for a few years, we set off in two cars and drove to the ferry port, parked on the ferry, and crossed to Calais. Then it was a long drive through France stopping occasionally for coffee and toilet breaks. We shared the driving with our other halves, and after a good eleven or so hours since leaving home, we arrived. The sun and tranquility was lovely. A quiet site set on the edge of the forest, with very little traffic.

Our children spent time with Jo's two children at the pool and we drank red wine and ate cheese and baguettes. It turned out that the landlady of Laurie's local pub also had a caravan in France. It was just down the road from us in Saint Tropez, and of course we paid her and her husband a visit, more jovial drinking was enjoyed.

I discovered that Laurie and his brother-in-law, Richard, had been very adventurous and active in their younger years. They had both

Chapter Fourteen

enjoyed mono water skiing at Grafham water and became pretty skilled at it. Richard also took his whole family snow skiing in France, though I'm not sure Jo enjoyed it.

When Laurie and I finally decided to get married, (once bitten twice shy for both of us), he accepted a friend's offer of a holiday in Bandung, Java. I'd been eyeing up Tobago but I think Laurie was excited to meet up with his old friend, Alan. I had met Alan previously when he had just started dating his wife Su. He was very chatty and she was more reserved.

I gradually warmed to the idea of a honeymoon in Java and embraced Laurie's adventurous nature to try out this unusual destination.

Laurie loved travelling and flying. Not just commercial flights either. He once joined a few friends on a private flight where his friend who was piloting the plane tried his best to make them feel somewhat queasy. The journey back was also no joy as in retaliation one of them let stink bombs off.

On another private flight to Europe, joining his friend Colin, he forgot his passport, and he woke me up with a phone call asking me to bring his passport to him. Not quite awake, I rummaged through his private cupboard for his passport, then I threw a coat over my nightdress, grabbed my car keys, and in my slippers drove off from Hitchin down the A1M to catch them up on the bridge over the motorway at Hatfield. I had no makeup, no sense of humour and needed a cup of tea desperately. He was very grateful and I was very tired. To make matters worse, he told me that when they landed in the private field set up for the spectators and their private planes, near the track of the Grand Prix, no one asked to see their passports.

Much later in life and coping with his many aches and pains, Laurie advised me that he was taking his motorbike test. "What! I thought you had already passed?" I exclaimed. Turned out he was so busy living it up and partying, he had not made time. Now he wanted to achieve this. Of course he passed and was thrilled. He bought an old bike and raced around our garden with me on the back. I decided that actually I probably wouldn't go on the road with him.

Our honeymoon to Bandung started the next day. I hardly slept. We were going for ten days, the dogs had already gone to the kennels and James, now nineteen, was house sitting.

Alan had asked us to bring a couple of pork pies and some port. Obviously hard to get in Indonesia at that time. We had bought some really nice pies and placed them in the fridge. Now we put them in a small cool bag and packed them into our cases. Once at the airport we bought the port and I think Laurie placed them into his cabin bag. You could do that in those days.

The flight was long and tiring. We landed at Kuala Lumpur airport where we had a few hours of waiting before boarding our next flight. We both smoked in those days and after such a long flight we headed for the smoking room within the airport. The experience was terrible, as soon as we neared the door, the smell was overpowering and choking. As someone came out, all you could see was a thick fog inside of the room. I decided not to bother, I may have been a smoker, but on this I drew a line.

After a couple of boring hours and withdrawal irritation, we boarded the flight to Jakarta. It wasn't long before we landed and went through customs.

Whilst struggling with our bags and hand luggage heading for the exit, one of the bottles of port smashed. Not a good start, but Alan and Su were there to greet us, and we soon cheered up as we headed off to a hotel in Jakarta for the night.

Chapter Fourteen

After a lovely shower and change of clothing we headed down for dinner. The hotel was beautiful, the food lovely. Kangaroo pie was on offer and wine and conversation flowed. Laurie took a picture of me sitting near the entrance later. I was trying to cool down and had not noticed until we had the photos developed back home, that a sign above my head read "Rent Me".

It was for surfboards, the sea being so close to the hotel, but Laurie of course knew exactly what he was doing.

We were all up early the next morning and after breakfast we took a look at the beautiful gardens around the hotel. Huge pots with trees in flower adorned the entrance. After a busy time at work and a busy time planning our wedding, it was so lovely to relax. Alan and Su had cargoed their own car from England when they came to Bandung. It was very comfortable, had good air-conditioning, and Su was driving us today. Some of the main roads were fabulous and strangely empty. Eventually we saw a sign telling us why. The South East Asian games were being held in Java, starting that very day. In fact some of the competitors had been on our flight.

We would soon be directed onto lesser quality roads which were narrow, not so well maintained and would wind their way upwards and around the hillsides.

Fast charging Indonesian buses came at us down the hill, as we drove upwards, our car clinging desperately to what road was being left to us by the buses. Su did an amazing job, Alan laughed occasionally as Laurie blurted out the occasional "bloody hell". I looked down the hillside to my left and had an amazing view of all the old, rusting, buses and cars that did not manage to stay on the road. They drive on the left hand side in Indonesia, nothing to do with England, simply a choice the country made. I could see the tea plantations and the hard working country folk below on the many hillsides. I deliberately focused on the beauty of the landscape to avoid watching overcrowded buses and motorcycles racing towards us.

As the roads became gridlocked, possibly because the main roads had been closed off, Alan said we should turn into a nearby village, have something to eat and drink and wait out the busy period.

It was a good decision and so we spent a while watching the local people go about their business, and the slow congested traffic driving past us. Then as the traffic cleared we set off once more. I'm not sure if Su continued driving or whether Alan took over the chore but we eventually pulled into their drive within the quiet town of Bandung.

As we parked, one of their house staff rolled a large metal gate behind us to secure the entry. It was a delightful house, and as soon as we entered, their lovely dog Luka came to greet us. I know nothing of the quarantine laws there, but it must have been fairly easy to bring a dog in at that time, a mere few days for Luca to be separated from them, and not the months we had to do in the UK at that time. A decade later I think Bali had a rabies problem, so things were probably tightened up after that, even in Java.

That first night Alan gleefully cut into one of the large pork pies. How he had missed their taste.

We were due to stay for 6 days with them, and then at their expense, we would fly on to Bali for a further 3 days. They were friends with a hotel owner there, and this final part of our honeymoon was a wedding present to us. Fabulous.

During our time with Alan and Su, we were taken to see an active volcano. The smell was unpleasant and small puffs of smoke rose up around those brave enough to walk towards the crater. A wooden fence helped to mark out the best way to indulge in a walk around the crater. Su had Luca with her so I stayed on the path they took. Laurie

Chapter Fourteen

of course entered the slightly more dangerous zone. Everything was black underfoot, but I remember beautiful, bright sunshine, making the scene before us seem safe and tranquil.

One day was reserved for being pampered. Laurie went off to have his hair cut with Alan. Su and I were having our nails done and were also given a facial.

Laurie was full of praise for his "best haircut ever". They had handed him a stein size glass of beer to enjoy as they went about their work, and gave a neck and shoulder massage at the end.

Su and I were also being massaged, our hands, our feet, nails painted, facial towels cleansing our skin. At one point the young Muslim girls left the room, at about three pm I think, and disappeared to pray. When they returned, they completed our beautification and we returned to the house to share our experiences.

On another day Su took me off to meet some other expat wives. To fill their day they formed book clubs, cookery classes and indulged in creative activities. The homes were always beautiful, with local help employed to do their gardens, the washing and cleaning. Su had taken it upon herself to write a book on all aspects of tackling how to live and enjoy Bandung. There was advice within the pages on money conversion, best restaurants, and much more. She and I had a fabulous lunch in a restaurant perched at the top of a hillside, overlooking splendid views. The food was amazing and the views even better. I think she was doing a review of this restaurant and I thought what a fabulous job to have.

After a few days Laurie and I decided that we would quite like to see the town center and have lunch out. Both Su and Alan were busy that day, but Su was very worried about our safety.

Anyway, we were dropped off in town and soon found a lovely park to stroll around. It wasn't long before the locals were coming up to us, entranced by our "moon faces" as they called us. One or two tried out their English on us. It was all very cordial. When we were ready, hailing a taxi, we managed to return safely and Su was visibly relieved.

It wasn't until four months later that I fully understood her concerns. The students ran amok in Java, attacking the foreign tradesmen in their country, overturning their wares and conducting protest marches. Alan and Su had to leave Java for their own safety, and had quickly packed up their home and left. Their car was again booked onto a ship and was returned once again to England. And dear Luca of course accompanied them. Obviously Su had been well aware of the political undercurrent, and feared an uprising at some point.

For the final three days of our honeymoon We were traveling to Bali and were booked into a fabulous hotel. The flight was short and rather basic, I was well aware of the plane being rather old and for most of the journey I wondered if we would make a safe landing.

We were picked up at the airport by the hotel bus and we pulled up outside of the entrance which was enormous. There were no doors at all to the front of the building, and as we climbed the gorgeous, wide steps and entered the hotel, it was vast. Ten foot, or perhaps 15 foot high statues of traditionally dressed men forming a circle were in the center of this reception area, set on a circular stage. I think they were carved from wood. In fact, highly polished, fabulous looking wood was everywhere. Staircase, steps, decorations and floors. The male and female waiters were all in traditional dress.

Succulent exotic fruits were placed in our room, and our balcony overlooked the hotel pool.

We were in paradise.

Chapter Fourteen

Our stay would be for three days so we enjoyed an organised trip out, a drive all around the island, a visit to a local village, and we bought masses of souvenirs when our driver stopped and invited us to go around the tourist stalls.

I bought tablecloths, napkins, coasters and one two foot tall carving of a bare breasted female plantation worker. As we were having lunch, a seller was cheekily waving to us clinging to a rock. The fall he was risking doesn't bear thinking about. Behind him was a wonderful scene of sunshine and blue skies with tropical greenery dipping down below him. Later, as we got into our air conditioned vehicle, he jumped onto the side of it as we set off. Laurie laughed and bartered with him. He gained money and we gained the carving of the plantation lady. I had to stick her in the centre of my suitcase to protect her on our journey home.

So we had finally tied the knot after twelve years together. My daughter was twenty two and my son nineteen,- I had brought us through divorce and illness on my own, reaching a point of calm in our lives and still remaining friends with my ex husband's family. Meeting Laurie was a concern, but his stoic character and ability to be inclusive made it easy for us.

I still gathered my own friends and my children's family around us and over the years we had so many parties and family dinners. Andrew and Sheila really liked Laurie and as a couple we became firm friends. After the court case in London my ex family took Laurie and I out to dinner to thank us for our efforts on their behalf.

Everything was going well for us. Our factory was becoming successful, Samantha was at university and doing well. We saw her get her degree, become a teacher, buy a house, and find love. James also flew the nest, buying his own maisonette and later finding love.

His passion was computers, often building his own from scratch. He ran his own company from an early age and helped many small firms or individuals take their first step into computerisation.

Laurie's brother was also doing well, and nine years before our wedding his first baby girl arrived, followed by twins a few years later.

Christmas now was an even bigger event. Boxing day saw all of Laurie's nephews and nieces mixing with my children, watching films together, and eating copious amounts of festive food. For a while we had Laurie's parents too, old and frail but able to enjoy all of their grandchildren in one place.

Truly lovely years.

We often shared holidays with other friends and family, and when my friend Myrtle and her husband decided to move to Spain, some years after our marriage, we would often leave our own place in Benalmadena, near Malaga, to hire a car, and travel for four hours to visit them for a day or two in Albox. Myrtle was lively, loud, beautiful, with short cropped hair and shiny brown eyes.

Her lipstick was always bright red and her nails were always immaculate and red too. She made regular visits to the manicurist unlike myself. I've always had strong, long nails, and it was easy for me to do my own shaping and painting.

We took my younger brother to Spain also, to celebrate his wife's 50th birthday. He too spent many happy times visiting our house, bringing his children and his lovely dog. One year he and his wife helped us to dismantle two very old garages adjoined to the house. We were gearing up to partially rebuild our home. More of that later.

Samantha married and we all enjoyed her wonderful wedding. Then James fell in love with a girl from Thailand. Her father was a typical

Chapter Fourteen

Englishman who happened to love living and working in Thailand. He married a quiet, intelligent Thai lady and had two lovely children.

James assured me that they were nice people. I wanted reassurance.

I had been quite poorly of late feeling depressed and lackluster. I didn't know at that moment that I would become increasingly more ill over time, as I had a failing thyroid.

It was suggested that I take a holiday, the children were going to treat me. It so happened that James's young lady was going to Thailand to spend time with her mum. She pleaded with me to go out there and be a guest of theirs at the family home. My daughter was worried about me and didn't want me to go, but I agreed in order to put my mind at rest about James's potential new family.

Chapter Fifteen

So here I was on a twelve hour flight from London heading to Bangkok. I loved Java, would I love Thailand?

The walk through the airport was a long one, at one point I had to run because time was ticking. I hadn't realised just how big this airport was. I stopped briefly to draw on my inhaler. I think I had given up smoking the year before, and indeed I never smoked again after breaking the habit, some twenty years now, but my lungs had not yet recovered and I was struggling.

The inhaler worked and I was soon settled in my seat, my mind wandered from how Laurie and the work would fair without my input, to this meeting with James's in-laws to be.

The plane was evenly filled with both Thai and European passengers.

Twelve hours later after getting some sleep, my plane landed. I found my bag easily, and came through their custom gate, wondering whether to turn left or right. Suddenly to my left, where metal barriers were holding a throng of people back, I saw Sarah.

Smiling, I waved and headed towards her.

I chatted happily with Sarah, we always seemed to get on well. Her mother smiled at me but offered no words in English. Strange I thought, as clearly both of her children being almost twenty years old and twenty two respectively, spoke wonderful English. And why wouldn't they, they had an English father and had attended American schools whilst in Bangkok. In fact Sarah's accent was American. I decided that the mum was either shy or waiting to see what she could make of me during my interactions with Sarah.

The mother was driving her own car, and we soon left the main roads in Bangkok and were turning down quiet side streets leading to her home. A maid opened the sliding metal gate for us and closed it again after we parked inside. Very like Alan and Su's set up I thought.

The house was amazing, highly polished wooden floors, wooden banisters leading upstairs. Sarah's maternal grandmother was living in a room on the ground floor. A silver haired smiling lady. I think there was a shower room downstairs as well as upstairs, Sarah explained that in this hot country even visitors might go for a shower, to refresh and be comfortable. The house was air conditioned thankfully, something I hadn't given any thought to, but which I soon became grateful for. That first night I was made very welcome, I handed a gift of a pair of earings to Sarah's mum. I had assumed wrongly that she would have pierced ears like Sarah who also had a pierced tongue as well as pierced ears, and possibly a tummy piercing too. Her mum had pierced ears but they had healed over with lack of use. She proceeded to try and push the stem of one earing through. Oh dear! I think she may have been pulling my leg.

Then, even though it was quite late at night, I was told a lady masseuse would be with us soon to give Sarah and I a relaxing massage.

Chapter Fifteen

The lady started with me. At one point she pressed on the main artery at the top of my leg, the groin area. When she released the pressure, I literally passed out.

It wasn't for long, but previous massages had not caused this effect. Soon we were off to bed for some much needed sleep.

At breakfast the next morning I noted that Kelloggs cornflakes had been purchased for me. Not something they would normally eat at all. Great laughter was caused when the lovely grandmother thought I was eating dry chicken flakes, because of the chicken image on the Kellogg's box.

Over the next few days I was treated to some fabulous meals both at the house and at wonderful restaurants. Sometimes we used taxis and sometimes the mum drove. We had a couple of shopping excursions in Bangkok. Truly memorable. In one store the escalators just kept going up and up, for floor after floor. There were two floors devoted to just jewelry.

But the final floor was simply mind blowing. It was covered in new cars for sale. I wondered how on earth they maneuvered the cars into position. A larger than normal lift for the cars was on the side of the building. Blimey! That was certainly a bit different.

On the street level we visited a couple of rather select jewelers. Needless to say, I didn't purchase very much.

After just a few days, Sarah and I had to pack a few belongings as we had been invited by her father, now estranged from her mum, to spend a few days on an island further up the coastline.

We had a taxi drive into Bangkok center, where we were dropped off at the bus stop. Here I met her father, a tall, thin, kindly looking

Englishman. He was not a man of many words but easy enough to get on with. After over an hour on the hot windowless bus we arrived at a building by the sea. Various tourists and passengers paid for their journey to, I assume, different islands. Our boat was not large, but pretty quick. Soon we had pulled up alongside other moored boats. Sarah and her father threw their bags onto their shoulders, and started to walk across the top of the sides of the boat, then onto the next boat until they could jump down onto the jetty. I was astonished, and on this particular day my feet were feeling like flat kippers with no feeling. I had still not been diagnosed with my low thyroid condition and was not at my best. The small Thai men who helped the passengers, began lifting me along the boats until I could also step down onto the jetty.

How embarrassing.

We then loaded the bags and ourselves into a jeep like vehicle and sped off down a dusty track towards our holiday chalets. We had three altogether, each one very luxurious with an open air shower. The land behind the showers was steep and covered in local plants, so not overlooked.

There were one or two restaurants to choose from along the beach, and a glorious infinity swimming pool which we made good use of.

I recall being a bit emotional on this two or three day break. Looking back, I think it was because I was relieved for James, they were a nice family, but also I was pretty poorly within myself.

It was a strange break for me as I hardly knew Sahra and didn't know her mum and dad at all. But their kind nature and expertise of hosting their own family from England, helped a great deal. Her dad came from somewhere near Birmingham, and his sisters and their families often visited him over the years. I could tell Sarah was glad to be with her dad, her life was mainly in England now, but Thailand was in her heart I felt.

Chapter Fifteen

After another couple of days back with Sarah's mum, it was time to return home. We had one last meal at a restaurant on the side of the river in the center of Bangkok. Magical!

On my return home it was confirmed that I had a low thyroid problem, I was put on a tablet to make up for the deficiency, and soon became my normal self.

Chapter Sixteen

This second phase of my life, since meeting Laurie, was by far the most enjoyable and rewarding. I loved my children, I had done everything I could to build a future for them despite many problems. They both married and had children. I was blessed with four gorgeous grandchildren.

Laurie was always good with my children, but he was amazing as a granddad.

Our first grandchild, Amy, was a delight. We couldn't get enough of her and like all new grandparents we doted on her. We worked hard through the week, then looked forward to family get-togethers at the weekend, when we could laugh and play like children ourselves, amusing this wonderful new human being.

Two years later Maya, James and Sarah's daughter, was born. Her arrival was pretty special for us as she was almost born at our house.

Poor James and Sarah had been to the hospital twice through the night only to be sent home each time. Exhausted, they came straight to us after the second incident, as we only lived five minutes from the hospital. James fell asleep in his old bedroom and I could hear poor Sarah moving about restlessly.

At one point I became aware that she had gone to the bathroom and hadn't come out for ages. I became really worried, frightened that she may need some comfort. I roused James then knocked on the bathroom door. Poor Sarah was in quite a state, trying to be brave and cope, but she was losing a lot of blood. "Call the ambulance James. Tell them to get here quickly, the baby is coming. You can't go in your car again."

The ambulance came quickly and Sarah, now comfortable and calm with expert help around her, went off to the delivery room. The staff were very apologetic to them as this had all happened within a couple of hours of them being turned away for the second time. As I waved them off, feeling stressed and concerned, a neighbour came up the driveway to see if all was well with Laurie and I.

I turned into Margaret Thatcher saying "oh it's fine, we're having a baby".

Maya was a delight for her parents and her grandparents. Her Thai relatives soon came to visit and of course Sarah's mum came to stay for some weeks.

Some months later Lily was born, Samantha's second child. Beautiful blue eyes and a fantastic personality. Amy seemed a bit taken aback, bless her, though her parents had done all the usual preparations for introducing a new baby into the equation.

I was in my element, work was going smoothly, and each weekend was a pleasure with babies all around us. I was buying baby clothes, toys, and within a couple of years watching delightful nursery nativity plays.

Chapter Sixteen

When Amy was only about four she was singing in a toddler choir at the church, a one off event, and Samantha invited Laurie and I to see her.

Oh dear, she saw us sitting in the pews and was so delighted, she ran to us and sat between us, refusing to rejoin the choir. It was highly amusing, but a bit disappointing for her parents.

Last but not least, young Leo came into the world. Our first and only boy grandchild. A lovely healthy boy, and once again his Thai grandmother came on a long vacation. During Sarah's pregnancy with Leo, I had been able to help with taking Maya to her nursery. I definitely loved this time of life which threw me back in time, as if I was a mum again, but this time with no worries and lots of warm family around. And Leo was another delight. So bright, kind and gentle. Laurie adored him.

As they grew up and started school, we began going on zoo trips together, holidays abroad, and taking train trips to anywhere just for the fun of it. Wonderful times.

It was now time to address our home. Our house had taken a back seat for over twenty years. We did convert the back porch and incorporated it within a brand new kitchen very early on. But apart from decorating each room very little else was done. We both loved gardening, Laurie mainly liked working with the sit-on-mower, petrol hedge trimmer, and a gravel leveler, which he made himself for the back of his mower. He would hitch it to the back of his mower, then zoom round and round the drive until any weeds became loosened and all of the gravel looked well raked and even.

So much of our energy, in the summer months, had been invested in making the boundaries of the garden dog-escape proof, and keeping the hedges and lawns tidy.

When family or friends came to the many parties and get-togethers in our large garden, they always loved the prettiness and seclusion as we were also in the countryside on the edge of my beloved Hitchin.

As a child I was brought up with a love of gardening. My father and mother had bought our family home when I was a toddler. We had a large house with double garages attached. There were outbuildings, a small stone building with tiled roof with a stable door pointing towards the five bar gate which exited the garden, and an attached outdoor toilet of the same construction with a full door to step in from the garden on the other side. I remember one of my uncles stabling his grey horse in there, when he stayed with us for a few weeks, and I can remember us periodically whitewashing the walls inside of both buildings. The toilet was kept immaculately, as my father insisted on using it if he was gardening. Very early on after purchasing the house, dad had converted one of the bedrooms into a smaller bedroom leaving the excess to be converted into our main bathroom. The new entrance door led onto the landing with the stairs straight ahead. There was already a bathroom upstairs, but it was pretty shabby and we never used it once dad had built and plumbed the lovely new one. The bin men of those days also cleaned out the outdoor toilets. This was about 1954. They would lift the metal bins of normal rubbish and tip them from their shoulders into the roll top trash vehicles. Then with large scoop shovels they entered the back of the toilet. A different roll top section of the lorry was used. When finished, a light dusting of pink powder was sprinkled, leaving the area disinfected and smelling rather nice.

Chapter Sixteen

The rest of the garden was laid to lawn at the beginning, followed by rows of potatoes, peas, beans and across the top end of the garden, several bushes of gooseberries, four different types. Red ones for jam making, small, sweet, yellow ones for eating off the bush, and medium size green ones for pies. Wonderful! Dad also loved growing flowers and we had all different types of dahlias one year.

I recall after a few years he bought a double hand push plough to make his work easier. He attached leather straps around my sister and my waist. Then after pushing the metal plough into the soil, we both had to pull as he pushed. It worked very well, and to be fair the soil was so good it turned easily.

One side of our garden had the tall sides of three cottages, dropping down to a four foot wall all the way along. The end of the garden and the other long side was planted with six foot hedges. There was a right-of-way the other side of the long hedge, where the five bar gate exited, leading to the farmer's fields.

In front of the outbuildings and just in front of our kitchen was an established rowan tree. Many times I climbed up this tree and swung my legs over a branch which stuck out at a right angle, swinging to and fro upside down with my hair dangling towards the ground. It rather terrified my mum but it made dad laugh. He knew I could handle it.

So at this early age I knew how to grow most things, and I knew the joy of harvesting and tasting fresh vegetables and fruit. For a couple of years my sister and I also went tattie picking for the local farmer. I earned five shillings for half a day, or ten shillings for a whole day. We had children's rates. I don't know what the older children and adults earned. Potato picking for the farmer was a little different to harvesting from our own garden.

You had to crack on, some potatoes were huge, and of course we witnessed babies and mother mice etc being churned up with the tractor's machinery.

So when we moved in with Laurie, into his home on the edge of Hitchin, harvesting the fruit from his apple and pear trees, and raking up leaves from the forty to sixty foot high deciduous trees (planted by the original owners in the nineteen thirties), -was to me a pleasure not a task.

Chapter Seventeen

My first husband, it seems to me, missed out on so much. His two wonderful children and now four grandchildren filled Laurie and my life with so much joy. Perhaps he was gaining those same happy feelings with his step children, I don't know. But because I kept in touch with my first in-laws I also had the pleasure of watching nephews and nieces flourish and have their own children. Since the court case, I don't think he was able to visit his family as he might otherwise have done.

As a family we now had to face some health scares. Laurie had already had open heart surgery, just a few weeks before Samantha married. He managed to walk her down the aisle, looking so pale and thin, but he did it.

He recovered very well. Then some time later he had a fall and broke his neck. This event kept Laurie in hospital for thirteen weeks. The consultants were not convinced that he had a break. Nothing showed up on the x-ray, mainly because his shoulders, affected by ankylosing spondylitis, were in the way of viewing the neck vertebrae properly. He became depressed, constantly wearing a neck brace and being told he could go home, even though he knew his head had dropped forwards. The work's manager and I were doing our best to keep the company going for him.

We had a very good friend called Peter who was an osteopath. A meeting had been arranged with Laurie's consultant, head nurse, myself and Laurie. Peter pointed out some questions we should ask which would alert those at the meeting that we would not be fobbed off and had a second opinion in line if need be. After the meeting they sanctioned an MRI which we had been calling for. At last a break the size and shape of a peanut showed up. They were so apologetic, within one day Laurie was transferred to the Royal Free hospital in London. He was fitted with a metal chin and neck brace, laced with straps across his shoulders, back and chest . Over a period of time, as his break healed, they would ramp his head up to take his chin off his chest. Poor Laurie, he had endured so much and now had more months of this to go. Friends and family had been amazing, visiting him in hospital and now also at home, for what turned out to be months.

A period of relative calm followed, health wise, and once Laurie was back into the swing of things, we began to do really well at work. Though not a fit man by any means, he would not retire, plus we turned our attention to improving our now very tired house.

Laurie had plans drawn up to replace our double garages with much larger ones, add a room behind them and also build on top of the structure. This meant changing the whole of our roof structure, not least because one of the down stairs original rooms had a flat roof. He decided to build on top of that too, and the new roof addition would incorporate all of these changes. A massive project.

Most of the house would have to be covered in scaffolding for many weeks to stop the rain from getting into the house.

Chapter Seventeen

Such a busy time followed, but he was in his element. I came home one day to find that my favourite room was now missing its ceiling. The flat roof had been removed and also two thirds of the front of the house forming this room was gone. All of the walls inside were gouged out in some form or other as electric cables and new plumbing was chased into the walls, heading upwards, to what would be our master bedroom and en suite. I was horrified, but Laurie and the builders found my reaction amusing. Really!!

About a year before this building work started, my younger brother and sister-in-law plus their dog, came down from Yorkshire to help us demolish the two old garages. They worked extremely hard, pulling tiles from the apex roof and sliding them down to be piled neatly below. The weather wasn't kind either. Their stirling work meant that some months later with the ground now clear, foundations could be laid for the new construction. Laurie's vision could take place.

After ruining my favourite room, the new brickwork began, and soon small walls became tall room sides.

Large timbers began to form a new, huge, roof. When the windows arrived and the roof tilers began their work, I started to relax. Soon the new floors would get their boards and we would be able to walk around the place safely.

Very soon the exciting part for both Laurie and I could begin. Choosing tiles for the bathrooms, the type of fixtures and furnishing for each one.

We were upgrading our family bathroom, gaining a downstairs walk-in shower room, an ensuite for our new master bedroom, two small shower rooms for the bedrooms above the garage and an extra ensuite for an older bedroom. From one bathroom to six, one of which would be downstairs. This poor tired house was now a modern stylish home worthy of still more parties to have, and to house all of our visiting grandchildren. Laurie and I had worked together through some tough times, and the house always had to wait, but now he could be proud of his vision and I felt that whatever happened now, we were secure.

The footings for the garages, which would also take the weight of the new bedrooms, were laid about ten months before the actual build began. So to have such hardworking tradesmen, completing their work speedily for us, was great.

We took our time to get the plastering and electrics done. The tiling was a big job, six new bathrooms, and every few days bathroom furniture arrived. Everything was painted then, though I did paper a feature wall for Amy's room. Our plasterer was not amused when he came back some months later to enjoy a celebratory bbq.

We enjoyed our beautiful home for almost three more years before terrible news was given to us.

Laurie had stage four lung cancer.

He had a cough and I was constantly asking him to see the doctor. He wouldn't. Then I joined him for a hospital appointment for one of his routine ailments. His consultant said that his blood results had shown one or two highlighted areas and wondered if Laurie felt well. I said he has had a persistent cough for a long time.

The consultant said "we will get an x-ray now" and he sent Laurie down the long corridor to the x-ray room.

Within half an hour, we were able to see the results and sure enough the cancer showed up.

Of course they didn't say cancer straight away, Laurie had to see more consultants, have more images taken, before it was confirmed.

Chapter Seventeen

He was so brave, we talked to the consultant with stiff upper lips using some inner strength. But sadness overtook us both once home, and I cried each time I left the room.

We had a holiday booked for Sri Lanka in three weeks time. We were treating Samantha, her husband, and their two girls as she was going to be forty very soon.

Laurie didn't want them to know, he didn't want to spoil her birthday treat.

The year before, my children's biological father had died, falling downstairs and breaking his neck. I went to each of their homes with Laurie to give them the news.

I was somewhat nonplussed to find that neither of the children took the matter to heart. They said how sad it was, but really after years of him ignoring them, they treated the news as if I was talking about a neighbour or a distant friend.

I was more affected, feeling sad at all that he had missed, not just his children and grandchildren, but his own siblings and their children. He paid a high price for his skullduggery.

The few weeks to our holiday in Sri Lanka soon passed, but I failed miserably to hide Laurie's condition. My daughter knew me so well that her concern for my "odd behaviour" as she called it, was threatening to mar our holiday. One week before we were due to fly I told her of Laurie's condition, saying "he wants to have chemo, he's going to fight. He has so much strength, he will be fine."

So we all set off with the usual holiday airport stress messing with our heads. The grandchildren were excited and oblivious, Samantha, her husband, and myself put on a show of strength and chatted happily to the girls.

The holiday, the sights, and the hotel were exceptional and we were able to put the sad news to one side briefly. Samantha and her family did lots of sightseeing, they did an organised elephant tour, and visited a turtle sanctuary. We joined them on a visit to the spice farm where we were shown how they gathered and peeled the cinnamon, and of course we bought some to take home. Samantha bought several of their traditional masks from another shop, each type used in dances for warding off evil, or healing various parts of the body, and some to tell the history of the various tribes.

Laurie treated me to a jewellry set of beautiful moonstone surrounded by tiny sapphires at a Sri Lankan gem mine. We saw how the miners entered the shafts, going down vertically for anywhere up to 60 meters. They create horizontal shafts either side of the main entry around two by four meters long. Nearly all of the mining is still done by hand, with pick axes and spades. The rubble they create is brought up to be washed in nearby rivers. It's a long and arduous process, but the few skilled mining families who still do this work, passing down their skills to each generation, are more than elated when gems are found. I did read that a few mines are sanctioned for machine work, but less impact to the environment is caused by the manual mining. These days, when a mine is finished with, they have to return the land to its original state.

I know for certain I could not go underground in that way. The entrances were tiny and they didn't have any protective gear.

One of my favourite excursions was the river boat trip which started on the river just outside of our hotel. We had to cross this river to get to our hotel when we arrived, and a trip to the local opticians for Laurie's glasses to be repaired also involved crossing the river.

Chapter Seventeen

The excursion was really good. As our low, flat boat with an engine on the back sped off from the hotel side, we were all smiling and ready for an adventure.

Our lovely guide was soon pointing out the long tail monkeys in the tree canopies. He cut the engine to cruise under some hanging fruit bats, and pointed out traditional single huts with local people going about their day. He got the children over excited and terrified at the same time, by scooping into the water and pulling out a baby crocodile. He proceeded to hold it on each of their shoulders for Laurie and I to take pictures of their rather nervous reactions.

The river became narrower the further we travelled, I loved the look of the tangled mass of long roots of the trees reaching out of the water, up to where the tree was finally situated. Our guide stopped the boat at one point amongst some of the tangled roots, and scooted barefoot along a fallen tree. I believe he had spotted a lizard and tried to catch it for us to view.

The trip was only for one hour but it was an amazing experience, and as we came out of the gloom of the enclosed river back into bright sunshine, there on the lush green lawns of our hotel grounds, was a black throated water monitor lizard. It was huge. It slowly walked across the grass, tongue flickering occasionally, so impressive. The children were so excited, and Samantha, whose fortieth birthday this trip was in aid of, couldn't have been more happy. She loved the whole trip. I do remember it with happy memories, of course, and I'm so glad that it was already planned, but each night as I sat with Laurie over our gin and tonics, his sadness mingled with mine and tears filled our eyes, our hands squeezing each other to offer love and support. It was so hard.

Once home we received a letter for Laurie's first round of chemotherapy. A set plan for the weeks ahead was given to us. Luckily it was going to be at the Lister hospital which was a mere five minutes from our home. Small mercies!

Many friends were supportive during this period, I recall our friends Keith and Angie coming over to sit and talk with us. Keith was born the same year as Laurie and was part of our social group known as the forty four boys. There were six men in this group and each one gave a party on their 50th, 60th and 70th birthdays. Fabulous events at different venues, which we all thoroughly enjoyed. I believe Gerry, another lovely friend, who started all the party celebrations with his wife Cathy, had a personal guest named Kiki Dee one year. She is a well known singer of the 1970s and she sang a duet with Elton John which I watched on "Top of the Pops", the song did very well at the time.

Unfortunately Laurie became ill after just one treatment. His years of taking a tablet aimed at helping his ankylosing spondylitis, had weakened his kidneys. He could no longer have chemo, they said.

By Christmas he was on a course of radiotherapy. He had a painful and weak time that Christmas.

At the end of January in the new year, he felt so much better. We planned a trip to our holiday apartment with all of the children and grandchildren plus a few friends for April. It went well and Laurie loved feeling part of life again. For myself, I struggled, tears were always so close.

When we saw his oncologist next, Laurie wanted to try out a new drug which involved immunotherapy. Our work manager had done some research, and also my own research, had pointed us in a

Chapter Seventeen

new direction. This oncologist was actually using the drug for private patients, but was unsure for Laurie.

We made the decision to visit a London clinic where this drug was being used.

We had a great consultation, but Laurie was now too weak, he had lost too much weight. They said we should get him to a hospice. That day our two wonderful friends Colin and Madeline, were driving us. We went straight to Laurie's local NHS oncologist who managed to get us into the Letchworth hospice the same day. Poor Laurie was exhausted by now.

What an amazing place. The doctors there did an assessment, they took him off some long standing tablets, gave him rest and good food laced with extra carbohydrates. He put on nine pounds in only two or three weeks.

Another patient there, also suffering from lung cancer, was given a place on a trial in Cambridge. The same drug that Laurie wanted. Laurie was visited by all the family and he was so boosted that he wanted to try the London clinic again. I took a photograph of him, now looking so much better. I sent it off with a text to the consultant. They were so pleased for Laurie. They organised his chemo and we made the decision to leave the wonderful Letchworth hospice. I was terrified, I think even Laurie must have wondered about this decision.

Surprisingly, the chemo did not have a bad effect this time, the consultant in London had assured us it would be alright. But why was it ok this time? I suppose I will never know.

There followed two or three more courses over the weeks, the last one culminated in Laurie being admitted to the Princess Grace hospital. The treatment was working but the cancer had damaged his lungs too much by now.

After several days, with Laurie's lungs failing, my daughter and I brought him home with oxygen.

The next day was bright sunshine with a slight breeze.

"Shall we go for a drive?" he said.

Standing in front of me in his dressing gown, with his oxygen connected, it seemed crazy.

"Alright" I said. "What about the tank?"

"It will be ok for a short time," he said.

I walked to my car, turned on the engine and pushed the button to remove the roof into the boot. I went back inside to guide Laurie to the passenger seat. His sight was quite a problem too now.

I drove us slowly out of the drive, turning right towards the country lanes, winding up and down and round the roads, not meeting any traffic. "What can you see?" I asked as I watched the breeze flutter his hair about his forehead. "Not very much" he answered.

I knew he was loving the freedom, traveling and driving still pleased him. I took in his facial expression, and smiled at the fact he was in slippers and dressing gown. He would never have left home, ever, without being well put together. Reluctantly, we returned home, he might have become cold and he needed his oxygen.

He was fine. For me it was the saddest day.

The next day, when I returned from a few hours spent at our factory, for wages day, Colin and Madeline, who were keeping Laurie company, reported that he was a bit confused.

I now know that the oxygen was not staying in the lungs, and was therefore affecting his brain. I will not go into the trauma of that night, when both of our children and myself sat with him, or the care of ambulance staff and a doctor, when palliative care was given.

Laurie, the love of my life, passed in his sleep in the early hours, at home, as he had wanted.

Chapter Eighteen

And so the third phase of my life began.

I have been on my own now for eight years. That is except for Buddy. My delightful, bossy, lively, Jack Russel. Shortly after we were told of Laurie's cancer, I mentioned to my daughter that I would like to get another dog. We had been without a pet for a couple of years, save for Percy parrot. I felt that we needed something else to occupy us in those sad quiet moments, when our minds strayed to thinking of the treatment and possible outcomes.

On our first visit to the Blue Cross Kennels at Kimpton, Buddy was shown to us as one of two possibilities. The other dog was a little girl with curly long hair. Buddy was six months old, he rushed into the room, jumped up onto a settee, then down, and cocked his leg on a table leg. He was clearly pretty stressed. I loved him. When they said he had no indoor manners and would probably always have a problem, I didn't care. The lady and Samantha did their best to dissuade me, pointing to the more sedate little bitch.

These days you have to visit your chosen pet a couple of times before leaving with them. They check out your home and family pretty thoroughly. On our next visit Laurie came too.

He reluctantly agreed to us adopting Buddy, so I went shopping for a new dog bed, new collar and lead, and various toys.

On the day of pick-up I was on my own. I felt the first rush of happiness that I had been able to feel, for quite some time.

Christmas was only a couple of weeks away, our son James and Samantha were taking Laurie for his radiotherapy appointments at Mount Vernon as they were evening appointments. We had planned to be alone for Christmas, as the treatments went right up to the day practically. We knew Laurie would need lots of rest and would probably feel ill.

Over the next days and weeks, dear little Buddy made us laugh and kept us on the go. I have a video of this dear little chap, jumping onto our bed, quite high for him, and grabbing one of Laurie's socks, just as he wanted to pull it onto his foot. Laurie started a pretend pillow fight with Buddy who stood on two hind legs and proceeded to box the pillow. He made us start our days with laughter and Laurie made the effort to walk him around our garden, rather than just sitting.

Once into the new year, I joined Buddy and myself up to "Barking Mad" for training and exercise. The site was fairly near to where we lived, and once a week I tortured myself around the obstacle course.

Buddy loved it, I on the other hand was sixty five with dodgy lungs. I was more than happy to give him this experience, and I think it helped greatly in breaking some of his bad habits.

I still had to go to work, especially on wages day. Our works manager, Cameron, had been amazing. He did his very best to keep quoting on potential work, we did deliveries between us, and we were so lucky as

Chapter Eighteen

a company, because we employed incredibly talented people, whose work was excellent. During the first six months of having Buddy, he had been amazing company for Laurie.

However, as Laurie became tired and began losing weight, I stayed at home more because Buddy's exuberance was too much for him.

Having Buddy at this time was also helpful for our friends. At difficult points in the conversation, they could pet him and we could all laugh at his antics. Pat Beaumont and her partner Peter, who helped us so much when Laurie was struggling to get the right help for his broken neck years earlier, came to visit us. Pat, a beautiful person, inside and out, brought toys for Buddy. He immediately started playing, throwing the toys up in the air and stretching up to catch them. He was like a circus dog twirling on his back legs and thoroughly enjoying himself. In front of him sat Laurie in his favourite, comfortable chair. "Pat, are you listening to me?" said an exasperated Laurie.

He had been trying to explain something to Pat, but she had completely collapsed into hysterics, whilst watching Buddy.

When I was a child we had a black collie named Rex. A popular dog name in those days and I remember walking him out of the back garden and up to the first field, just behind our back garden hedge. This field belonged to a farmer who lived on his own.

There were one or two abandoned horse jumps, quite low, and I used to run with Rex and encourage him to jump them. He was really pretty good. The farmer's wife had died some years earlier and he became somewhat reclusive. Despite popping into his field many times, I never saw him, although on a previous occasion, as part of the village scrumping gang, I certainly did see him. He was angrily shaking his fist at us all. We scrambled down and ran for it. Some of the kids turned and poked out their tongue, but I was red and embarrassed. I wondered if he might complain to my parents.

When my parents' noisy arguments were too much to bear, I used to go into Rex's shed, an outbuilding, and cry quietly holding him around his lovely furry neck. He was very empathetic and leaned into me, flicking his tongue on my cheeks to clear my tears.

I remember being devastated at losing him to old age and blindness.

It seems to me in writing this book, that I have always turned to a furry friend in difficult times. After James was born, and having been left the first time by my errant husband, I brought Max home. A tan and brown, Alsatian-Airedale mix. Such a gentle, happy breed. He was already three years old, a rescue dog. Around his neck he was framed by a thick, long, mane of hair. This earned him the description of "lion" dog.

At Hitchin he was loved by my neighbours, we lived in a maisonette then, there was no garden, just communal spaces. One couple would invite him into their home for biscuits, and the toddlers on the estate could often be seen sitting with him on our outdoor stairway. Some of the smaller ones crawled over him. I was always vigilant but never worried. When the children and I moved to Letchworth, we gained a garden where I grew potatoes, runner beans, sprouts, carrots and lettuce. Max loved it but escaped from a left open gate one day. When he came back he had an enormous joint bone in his mouth. He had made his gums bleed from the effort of getting it home. I was mortified, where did he get it from??

A week or two later, I found out. We walked Max down to the outdoor splash pool, after we finished there I walked us across the road to a butcher on the corner of the street, near the railway bridge. As I placed my order, one of the men asked if the dog held by my children

Chapter Eighteen

was mine. Then he said that Max had sat outside one afternoon, for a long time, and only left when one of them gave him a bone. Oh dear, naughty boy! We were all amused by this so perhaps he was more a clever boy.

When we moved in with Laurie and merged our families, Max had to get used to his two dogs. The two runaways!! They were always escaping. Laurie never had them neutered, and he spent hours some days looking for them. Once when Cass escaped, he managed to mount one of the pedigree bitches at a farm on the northern edge of our village. We received a call to collect Cass from the owner, who very annoyed at what had happened. Apologising profusely, we paid for a morning after pill, which their vet sorted out for their labrador. Our dear Cass, also a black labrador, was definitely not of decent enough breeding descent for them to contemplate a "wait and see approach." We eventually managed to fence the whole perimeter of our acre garden and solved the problem.

Now that I was on my own, I was so glad to have Buddy. Over the years, we had lost our first dogs, born the pain of grief of losing them, and eventually gained new dogs. They too passed, as Laurie and I approached thirty years of being together.

So we had been without a dog for a couple of years when we took Buddy on. Sadly he was only eighteen months old when he suddenly had to watch and hear my crying and feeling the pain of grief.

I couldn't go to Barking Mad with Buddy anymore as I had no sparkle or energy within me.

It took a year to sell our business and also the house, I couldn't grieve properly as work was now tough to handle. We missed Laurie's expertise and input, but with hard work and good men we got through and managed a sale.

I was rattling around our beautiful six bedroom home, so lovingly modernised by us only six years earlier, so I decided quite quickly to sell and find something smaller.

I wanted to stay in bed and hide away, but I went into work every day, taking poor Percy parrot with me. He was missing Laurie too. I did house viewings near to where my daughter lived, near Raunds.

Nothing inspired me. I looked at everything that came onto the market in Hitchin and nearby. I even looked at properties in the North of England, thinking I needed a fresh start.

I couldn't see it then, but I was lost.

I just knew that I couldn't stay where every building or person I saw was a memory of Laurie. People over time have described their grief as like "a kick in the stomach". Well that was exactly how it felt to me for a very long time.

Eventually, seeing me struggle with my new home search, Samantha came to the rescue. I told her I was always going to be lonely living on my own, that I wondered how she felt about me being in a granny annexe with her family.

I felt that this option was a good solution for many other worries that I had regarding my family. I could be a help rather than a hindrance, after all, despite my mental malaise I could still drive the car and wield the hedge trimmer, and cook some family dinners when required.

Chapter Nineteen

The home we found was in Staffordshire, near Uttoxeter. It was a large six bedroom home, and my annexe was joined on to the home at the end of a high vaulted, double conservatory. A door into a passage from my house, led to the conservatory and then to the main home.

Samantha and her family moved in at the end of August 2017, but I couldn't move until the second week of December. The paperwork seems to take the solicitors forever to complete. I was so lucky to have the same solicitor who helped me with my divorce and fighting nan's will twenty years earlier. But he still had to deal with others, and the searches, which on a large, older property, are a nightmare.

At first with so much to do, I settled quite well. I didn't have to go to work anymore. I was sixty six and had only ever had two or three months off work with paternity leave for each of my two children. I had started work at sixteen, and apart from normal holidays I had worked for fifty years. I must admit that the last ten of those years were perhaps an easy ride. No children to worry about, and a computer doing the hard work of my bookkeeping.

After planning the layout of furniture in my barn/granny annexe, it wasn't long before I was comfortable and happy. I can honestly say that I didn't miss work in the slightest. I got to see my grandchildren every day instead of every two or three weeks. They loved coming down through the conservatory to see me. Sometimes I could just hear them playing as I pottered around my kitchen. They had made part of the conservatory their playroom.

I had the bright idea of putting blackout material across two large side expanses of the window panes, and hanging a large projector screen at the end which was a brick wall and not glass. We created a quite large cinema room. The girls loved it, and bought popcorn for their evening shows. Of course they were still only twelve and nine years old at this point.

Once we were settled I seemed to get through the first summer ok. I went back and forth to Hitchin regularly to see James and his children. I would often be invited to stay with my friend Pat overnight, the lady who collapsed in laughter at Buddy's antics that time. She made me feel comfortable and always produced lovely meals. We did have a good laugh, and also many tears over Laurie.

Then as winter approached, I didn't do so well. I couldn't drive back to Hitchin, as the weather often made the two hour journey seem a bit treacherous for me. One accident and suddenly you are in a queue for four or five hours on the M1.

I became "the sewing repair lady", mending all the toys and family garments. They seemed pleased and I was happy to be useful.

I bought a very good camera, and took up a hobby that I had wanted to do since being a very little girl. Bird photography.

Chapter Nineteen

When I was only about eight, I was upstairs looking through the landing window at my tree for swinging on. A delightful, medium sized bird landed, singing away, and I stopped and stared at it for ages. I don't recall at all what type of bird it was, but I knew in that moment that I wanted to photograph it.

I harped on about getting a camera though I knew nothing of quality at that early age. My dad had a very good camera himself which had a tripod and a timer on it. Many a time he set it up and then raced around to our family group, just in time for the camera to capture an image of us all.

I was eventually bought a plastic "box" camera, a toy really, on display in a newspaper shop in Shildon. Even at that early age I knew it wasn't very good, but I began taking pictures of swans and people when on holiday.

Surprisingly the pictures turned out pretty good. I had the occasional blurry image, but no cut off heads, or black emptiness. This kept me happy for a few years though the cost of developing the pictures, plus getting to a town where the developer's shops were, meant I was limited in my progress. Also I couldn't zoom in with this camera so it was no good for bird photography. After that, life and children took all of my time. Now retired and with loads of free time, I was in my element.

Our new home was in the countryside. We had so many different birds visiting our garden.

I could easily zoom in on the birds of prey, resting on the fencing around the fields, or on high branches, as they looked down for their next meal.

I was able to download the images I took onto my laptop and make small movies with music. I was so happy and pleased, I started boring friends and Facebook with a few images of the birds. Once, in the field ten feet from my bedroom window, a duck popped his head up in front of me. Hardly awake, I grabbed my camera and took a few shots.

The next day I looked out especially for him, but as there was no water around this field I didn't really expect to see him. Yet, after a few minutes, there he was again, and unexpectedly another head popped up. The grass was very long and so all I had was a good head and neck shot, but what made it special was that after looking at themselves, they both turned their heads 180° looking over their own backs and it made for a super comical photo.

My youngest granddaughter Lily, was learning to play the ukulele. She did so well that I bought her a very nice wooden ukulele, as the schools only provided plastic ones.

We had hours of fun together composing music and lyrics. One song in particular, about saving our world from global warming was very good. We made a video of her performance of that one.

I wasn't surprised at all by this talent, (Samantha played the piano well, and James played guitar), because my first husband and his family were all talented musicians.

One of my children's cousins, Charlotte, was excellent on the clarinet, and today I often get to see Maya sing her own songs, accompanying herself with her guitar, in Letchworth town centre. Amy does not perform live like Maya, but she has an amazing voice. She can really sing anything. From Amy Winehouse vocals, Ariana Grande songs, (without the whistle note).... to big belted out show tunes.

In fact my own cousin who must be seventy or so now, has been the lead singer of a tribute band for years, with quite some success. My own mum could play her piano very well. In my first year of

Chapter Nineteen

marriage to Graham, he managed to teach me a couple of tunes on his guitar. I wasn't very good.

Another delightful pastime for me was my fish. I had kept a tank of fish for some years at our family home.

When I moved, I was down to just one little fish, who travelled to Staffordshire with me, his bag of water propped up on packaging on my passenger seat. I set up the small tank and he lived on for a few more months. Then I packed the tank and pump away as my interest dwindled for a while.

One Spring, my interest renewed and I set up a half barrel outdoor tank. I placed a brick inside, a long log for creatures to use if they fell in, and after the addition of gravel and pond plants, I bought three baby goldfish.

This tiny patio pond survived four or five years and endured the cold winters. I used to wrap the barrel in layers of bubble wrap in the winter. When I had to abandon this pond, I gave the fish away to a local shop whose owner sent me a lovely picture of them thriving in her indoor tank.

Life was just beginning to improve with my new found hobbies, my gardening, and being surrounded with loving grandchildren, who by the way adored Buddy, when Covid 19 arrived. This dreadful virus, and how it was handled by the world leaders, saw people dying and others left isolated for more than a year. The effects were devastating for everyone. The young had their education disrupted and were so fearful of giving their grandparents the disease. The old declined quicker than they might have, and it was a kind of torture for families not to be able to visit their older parents in the care homes. At Covid 19's peak, when people died, the government drastically reduced the number of mourners who could attend a funeral. The Queen, bless her, was a tragic, lonely figure at Prince Philip's funeral, because of these restrictions.

I sat on my own so much, unable to make connections with new friends or groups, which by now I needed to do.
After nine months of isolation, with occasional outings and being able to mix as a family within our large home, the worst happened. It was Christmas, we all gathered in Samantha's living room to open presents. So much laughter and fun. Then my son in law cooked the Christmas dinner and I left to get dressed before once again trotting up to their dining room.
We had a normal, happy time, with the usual alcohol and Christmas games and films going on. The cinema room we had created got full use. I went to bed feeling normality was returning to our lives.

Late the next morning Samantha was on the phone to me. Her husband's work colleagues had phoned. Most of them were ill with Covid. Samantha said we should all stay apart and wait to see if we became ill.
That night her husband became sick, then Samantha and the children succumbed by the next morning.
I have no idea how I did not catch this from them, but I didn't. They said it was horrendous. The chest pain felt terrible, and the lack of energy was the worst part. It must have been three or four weeks before we dared to meet in the conservatory, windows and doors thrown wide open. Even our dogs were kept apart in case we stroked the virus on and off their coats.

Chapter Nineteen

During this period I turned seventy, and like so many other people at that time, I would be on my own.

I embraced the day, so after a shower, I put on a fuchsia pink jacket over my dress, added makeup with fuchsia pink lipstick, and titivated my hair. I opened a bottle of sparkling wine and then James rang. Oh my goodness! He had organised a zoom call with family and friends. I seem to remember that after ordering me to turn on my laptop, he then took it over remotely, and did all that was necessary to connect us all. I was so glad that I had made an effort with my appearance, and it was an absolute joy to speak with everyone. I had received cards and presents via the post, and was now cheered by personal messages from those closest to me. Wonderful.

And so another Covid year started.

People were going out more. We all kept our distance in shops, we wore face masks everywhere. As we neared the end of a second year like this, people were getting pretty fed up. Loads started being mask free through the town streets. Many more were meeting up outside for social events. The government, with their daily updates, were just as adamant that we must comply with the rules.

Then just before we were about to enter another Christmas and New Year, we all found out that our politicians were the worst rule breakers. Partygate and more was reported in the newspapers.

So 2022 began with a lot of anger but also with the Covid rules being slowly relaxed. By June most of the restrictions were over.

In my world, I was happy to go out again. I was aware of how chunks of education had been messed up for my grandchildren and I was saddened to hear that many of my friends still wore masks when shopping. The fear of this disease had a real hold on many people even into the following year.

After such a horrible Covid period and with so much time alone to contemplate how life would return to normal, I rationalised that I was still too young to be living in a granny annexe. During 2017, I was exhausted from the effort of selling the family home and the business. I had stifled the grieving process and was easily persuaded by my own thinking process to join Samantha and her husband on a fresh start. I knew that I could offer so much towards helping with the children, as Samantha suffered terribly with a condition called fibromyalgia. However, six years had now passed and everything had changed. Amy had passed her driving test and both girls took care of themselves, spending more time with their friends than with the adults.

I wanted to go back to Hitchin, I wanted to see if I could start again, and to see if my friends were coping after such terrible times. It seems that Samantha and her husband were doing their own fresh appraisal of the situation too. He had changed his job a year or so before Covid arrived and was doing really well. A move nearer to his job seemed likely, so when I said I wanted to sell my barn to move back to Hitchin, it was decided that we would place the main house up for sale too.

There followed a long drawn out period of house buyers traipsing in and out of both of our homes. When a suitable house was worth viewing, Samantha would drive South to take a look. Similarly, I was going up and down the M1 every few weeks to check out properties.

One buyer of our home failed at the last minute to complete the process, and we had to start again. Both Samantha and I lost preferred houses and vowed to stop looking until we had another definite sale. It was an incredibly stressful time, I was the main gardener, and I spent a whole year trying to keep the garden extra tidy.

Chapter Nineteen

Samantha's husband hardly had time to relax at weekends, as the lawns always had to look great.

Was this move going to be worth all of this stress? I did love my barn. I loved the garden. But as the children were now so grown up, Amy was already driving, having passed her test and bought a car, I knew that I didn't want to be living with just my daughter and her husband.

Chapter Twenty

So after sixteen long months, tired and stressed, I stood in my new kitchen looking out at a flat black mess of soil. There was a garden shed in one corner and a few slabs to step out onto. It was the 28th April 2023.

Buddy was not impressed. I couldn't let him out as the clay soil squashed between his toes, and he wouldn't let me touch his paws. So on the first occasion he escaped, it meant hoisting him up in the air, holding him in front of me, and placing him in the sink to wash away the soil. Yeuk!

Of course I had foreseen this problem, and even before money was exchanged on my moving day, I had hired a landscape gardener to create a lawn as soon as possible in May. If things did not proceed I could cancel. In any event everything went to plan, and so I spent three weeks walking Buddy all around the estate, anywhere except my garden.

I had found a couple of lovely houses over the months of house searching, with established gardens. Sadly, their upward chains left me with both uncertainty and long wait times. As it was, buying this new build home still saw me storing my furniture for a month.

On my moving day I left Buddy with my friend Pat. We had come down a few days earlier to be fresh with energy for the moving day. Pat has always been there for Buddy and I and it was great to spend some time with her, taking the odd solicitor and agency calls as everything came together.

It was a wonderful experience placing my furniture in every room, knowing I had no cleaning to do beforehand. The carpets were brand new and everything was painted white.

James and his partner Louise helped me unpack and put away all of the crockery, glasses, ornaments and books. Curtain rails went up the next day, and a new light for the living room and a large rug, completed my main space. I had ordered online weeks before, and had the lights, rails and rug delivered to James.

It seemed within a week that I was settled. Buddy just needed that garden space then he too would be fine.

I had drawn a scaled plan of how I wanted the garden to look. The small patio was to be removed and replaced with a circle of autumn brown Indian sandstone slabs, with more slabs either side of the circle.

Then I would grass over the rest, cutting out various flower beds.

By the end of May the landscape guys finished their work on my plan and with the help of my friend Pat, the garden looked lovely.

I certainly could not have planted all of the flowers in one afternoon, which I had purchased, but with Pat's help that's what happened. Charlie Dimmock eat your heart out.!

Buddy wasted no time in enjoying the garden and as the rolls of grass settled and the new plants thrived. I knew I was going to be happy here.

Chapter Twenty

The clay soil would be a challenge but this was the smallest garden I had ever had so it would be a doddle.

My biggest problem was my weakened leg muscles. Six years of no stairs and cleaning my much smaller barn conversion, and two years in lockdown had left me feeling like a rather sedate old woman.

I realised that I was having to pull on the stair rail somewhat. I became breathless with very little activity. Now sixteen months later I'm fine. With such a small garden I have to do more walks with Buddy, and such is the improvement that I may have staved off a second hip operation.

My first hip operation, eleven years previously, had gone very well. Of course I had Laurie to help and spur me on then. He made supports for the settee legs, so that when sitting down the settee was at least six inches higher. He also stabbed me with the blood thinner injections after the operation once home, as I could not face doing them to myself. He was a bit too eager and happy to do them I thought! My daughter was able to help with the injections too I remember.

The summer months in my new home brought me to life again. My patio doors were always open that summer and into autumn it seemed to me. All of my friends were and are so welcoming. I was happy to see them and popping out for a coffee has become the norm.

Sadly, since returning, Laurie's sister has passed away, but I did manage to see her in her care home a few times. Her lovely children phone and visit me occasionally, and I meet up for a coffee when they are not too busy.

Lisa in particular is always on the go. She has four kids, mainly grown up now, and at University, but she still has loads to do for them, plus she has a full time job.

I still remember when I first started dating Laurie, Lisa and her friend were walking towards Laurie and I in Willian. It was the village fete day and Laurie was so happy to see her. It was either her birthday, or she had just had her birthday. She was thirteen and uncle Laurie was happily placing money into her hand for getting a treat. She had such a pretty happy face.

I now had to get used to neighbours again. For the last thirty eight years I had lived practically isolated with fields and trees around me. At least in my last home I had my daughter and grandchildren within shouting distance. When I was younger and going to work everyday, I hardly knew our nearest neighbours. If we had a party going on, we always invited them, and so gradually over the years a relationship was built with them. Laurie was notorious for being a good host and it was not unusual to hear in the following days that as our neighbours walked home, at least one of them would stumble into a bush. Indeed Laurie himself had left friends' homes after a good party, and found himself in a bush or two. I don't drink much, I was always the driver, so I managed to avoid falling into various bushes.

In my new situation, all of the neighbours that I have met, I really like. They work so hard, and the new homes are so well soundproofed that it is a very quiet estate.

My ex, step mother in law is now only fifteen minutes from where I live. In her nineties now, her mind is still very alert and caring. She, along with my friends, has made my return to the area a good experience. We rarely talk now about Graham, but I find it amazing to think that we have been friends for some fifty three years. Graham's twin brother Alan and sister-in-law Janet, are also held deeply in my heart. I suppose it could be the huge amount of years that I have

Chapter Twenty

known them, but they are always there and always kind when we talk. Although I moved on after Graham left us, they were, in my mind, still my family, adopted after leaving my own family, all those years ago. Laurie's family were in my life for many years and we have so many happy memories, but I have a deep and enduring affection for my first in-laws.

We rented homes near each other when first married, we shared the grief of losing their mother so early in their lives. A beautiful lady to look at and to be with. We had our babies together, fought a legal case together and all struggled to understand Graham, before letting him go his own way.

This third phase of life is the most challenging mentally I think. Friends and family are older and we all have health issues of one sort or another. It's lucky that the sense of fun in the people I know is so wonderful. We have drive and energy still, even if it's only in our heads.

The Letchworth girls, as I call them, spent two years of lockdown doing a morning walk around local fields.

It was amazing to me, as I sat all alone in Staffordshire, to hear of the morning walks. It brought the girls closer together, if that were possible. Through terrible stories and events with Covid, they had each other. They got fresh air and exercise, it kept them going. Some would not make the walk one day but then others could, and so their daily walk has outlasted the outbreak. They still go on their walks even today.

Tough times have affected most of us, sometimes affecting our own children now, who are late forty or fifty years old. How did that happen?

We got through our own difficult times and now we go through theirs. Thankfully, as with all things, it's mainly good news. The success of our grandchildren. Their ability to drive now and University successes. Pat Beaumont and I have both proudly watched our own grandchildren singing and playing guitar in Letchworth town centre.

When I was pretty young, maybe about nine, I really can't be sure, my dad, perhaps having a melancholy day himself, produced a picture of his mum.
She was in a Victorian style dress with pulled back hair and had an air of being well off. "This is my mum." he said.
"Her name was Jane, I named you after her," he said.
I remember feeling that this was important but as I always knew my name was Eileen Jane I just accepted his statement. As mentioned earlier dad lost his parents at a very young age and on this occasion I could feel his sadness but I was too young to understand.

At nineteen, when planning my marriage to Graham, my mum had misplaced my birth certificate. I sent off a request for a copy to Somerset House, who used to hold such records many years ago.
The church needed this for our marriage records to be filed.
When I received the paperwork, there was an A4 document and a smaller copy within an envelope. Both of the documents stated that my name was Jane Marshall. I was shocked, there was no Eileen mentioned within the documents. I suppose that was what my dad was trying to tell me.

I continued through my life using Eileen, but I have always been secretly pleased to know how Jane was chosen. Especially as I had personally struggled with my relationship with my father. This was an unbreakable bond in my mind. Indeed the name Jane has been passed to my daughter as a middle name, and two of my grandchildren have

Chapter Twenty

it as their middle names. I know my dad would have been thrilled to know this. I wonder what my mum thought. There were so many unexpressed questions by me during their later years. I never wanted to "bring things up" which might have upset them.

As I wrote the last few words of this book, a flashback of when we drove north to show my parents our new born first child, Samantha, entered my thoughts. I realised that at their home, as dad held Samantha Jane in his arms, I had of course told him her name!

I have lived my whole life, like most people, doing my best and overcoming hurdles. From fear and sadness, then losing some of my hearing, I took everything in my stride going forward.

After such a full and adventurous time, from difficult beginnings to a complex journey through my life, I am now looking forward to a wonderful continuation of this third phase. I'm sure it will be up and down and health permitting I'm ready for it. I may be called Eileen but in my heart I'm Jane Marshall.

www.ingramcontent.com/pod-product-compliance
Lightning Source LLC
Chambersburg PA
CBHW041308110526
44590CB00028B/4282